Prayer:
The Master Key

Prayer:
The Master Key

JAMES DILLET FREEMAN

DOUBLEDAY & COMPANY, INC., GARDEN CITY, NEW YORK
1968

*The author acknowledges with grateful thanks
permission from Unity School of Christianity
to use certain material in this book which orig-
inally appeared in* Daily Word.

CONTENTS

1437885

There is a deep pool

CONTENTS 9

CONTENTS 9

CONTENTS — 9

Prayer:
The Master Key

There is a deep pool in the heart,
and he who drinks of it is wise,
though not with the wisdom of the world.
He may not carry on a conversation with scholars
but he knows many truths that trouble their minds.
For he has drunk a living water
and its taste is very good.

Ask him questions, all you learned doctors,
and he answers you
not with lightning words
or hilltop thoughts
but from the perfect peace
that overflows
out of the deep pool
of his being.

I

A KEY TO A MYSTERY

✑ *I hunger and I thirst* ✎

I came to the Master as I wandered in the desert, and I said to the Master, "I hunger and I thirst."

The Master held out his arms to me as if to draw me to his heart.

But I stretched out my beggar's bowl and my empty cup and cried, "Food, Master, food—or I perish!"

So the Master raised his hand and lowered it again, and in my beggar's bowl were loaves and fishes and in my empty cup was wine.

I ate and drank. After I ate and drank, I slept.

But after I slept, I woke. Again I found myself wandering in the desert, and again I came to the Master.

I said to the Master, "I hunger and I thirst."

The Master said, "Give heed unto me."

But I cried, "Food, Master, food—or I perish."

Then the Master lifted up his eyes and lowered them again. The desert blossomed as a garden, springs gushed from the naked rock, and the whole land became as a land of milk and honey.

Then I went to and fro in my land. I ate and drank and slept. Among my fields and flocks, I dwelt and waxed fat.

So one day, full of food and drink and sleep, as I wandered in my land of milk and honey, I came once more to the Master. He sat silent. He did not move his hand. He did not speak. He did not look at me through his heavy-lidded eyes.

Then I fell down, and I said to the Master,

"I hunger and I thirst."

✺ *In the midst of a mystery* ✺

Life has set me down in the midst of a mystery.

It seems beyond my fathoming.

Yet I wake and look around me and hear, as it were, a voice saying,

"Seek and you will find. Ask and it will be answered. Knock and it will be opened."

So I seek and I find. But what I find is yet more to seek.

I knock and doors open. But every open door leads to yet a further door at which to knock.

I ask and I come on answers. But every answer is itself another question.

So I see that it is in seeking that I find, and in asking that I am answered.

For the meaning of the mystery—at the point where I can lay hold of it—is contained in the search and the question.

Life has given me a mind to ask and a spirit to seek and hands to knock at its doors.

Yet this much I see clearly—the mystery is not mystery because it is meaningless but because it is meaningful. It is not because things have so little meaning, but because they mean so much that I cannot grasp the meaning.

How shall an inchworm comprehend a continent?

But let the inchworm measure the mystery of a leaf or two, and it may turn into a butterfly and master even the mystery of air.

And if an inchworm can turn into a butterfly, who shall say what a butterfly may become?

I am God's inchworm and God's butterfly.

O God, I inch my mind across the mystery that is my world, measuring it as best I may. Sometimes, if only for a moment, I encounter a meaning that is like Light and an assurance that is like Love.

Then, though I cannot see the meaning clear, I know that whatever the meaning is, it is not less but more. And whatever I am, I am more, too.

⪧ *The key called prayer* ⪦

Life has set me down in the midst of a mystery.

But life has given me a key.

The key is in my own mind.

The key may not take me to the end of the mystery, but it takes me to the beginning.

Having begun, I can go on.

Having taken the first step, I can see to take the next step.

The key life has given me I call prayer.

You may call the key thinking.

Prayer may be thinking.

Thinking may be prayer.

Prayer, to me, is taking thought—but a special kind of thought.

Prayer is a thinking that is more like listening than like speaking.

Prayer is a thinking that sets the mind free. It does not tell the mind what to think; it asks the mind what to think.

Prayer tills the field of the mind.

It plows and harrows and sows; it waters and weeds.

But the mind itself brings forth the green and living thought out of its invisible amorphous depths.

The formless mystery shudders into form, and I exclaim, "Look, a rose!"

For the shapeless is forever seeking shape.

The unseen is forever becoming the seen.

The unknown and unknowable is forever becoming the known.

Prayer is the process of mind by which the unknowable finds meaning and becomes a truth; the unseeable takes shape and becomes a thing of beauty; the immeasurable gains substance and becomes a matter of value.

⪧ *A way of thought* ⪦

Prayer, then, as I treat it in this book, is a way of thought—yet more than a way of thought.

Prayer focuses thought on God the way a compass keeps its needle turned on North.

If I am a traveler, I carry the compass with its needle turning always North, not only when I want to go North, but so that wherever I have to go, I can find the way.

With my thought God-centered, I can go in any direction from that center and not be lost. Though I may not always see my destination, I can find my way.

But it is as true to say of prayer that it is longing as to say that it is thought.

It is as true to say that it is passionate involvement in life.

Prayer is always a reaching beyond ourself toward something greater than ourself.

We may feel that we reach in or out, but always beyond ourself.

Prayer is as much a way of the heart as of the mind and involves the body no less than spirit.

Prayer is the way of the whole man.

I pray when I give the whole of myself to God—or to truth or to beauty or to life or to love or to joy—whatever you prefer to call God or whatever name He may have chosen to reveal Himself by at the moment.

For God Himself is the mystery in which I am set down.

O darkness, are you, then, light—but light so blazing bright that I am blinded by you and must see you only a thought's glow at a time.

Immensity, are you compassion?

Everlasting God, are you my first faint glimmers of truth?

We do not need to know what the sun is in order to see by its light.

It is with God as it is with the sun.

We cannot clasp the vast and flaming orb, but we can live in its warmth a day at a time.

Prayer is my way that I lay hold of Infinite Perfection—a prayer at a time.

II

RELIGION IN OUR TIME

❧ *The origins of belief* ❧

I said to the Master:
"Is prayer the search for God?"
The Master said:
"What is God?"
Men have believed in God as long as they have been men.
They believe in God out of their own nature—because they are
what they are and the world is what the world is.

Something they see and experience in the world, something
they feel about life and themselves cries out to them that there is
a power or powers beyond their own that somehow they can
contact, and when they do they will have help.

A couple of hundred years ago learned men—set free from
ancient superstitions by the new scientific enlightenment—told
each other that men had invented God.

God—they said—is a super-sort of social sanction: Ancient
priest-kings who had the responsibility of government had invented this all-wise, all-powerful law-giver who had given society
its rules of order, the laws men are asked to live by. These priest-
kings had made up the story that they had gotten the laws from
Him in order to make the laws seem more lawful.

But man did not invent God; God invented man—man is
God's invention.

The belief in God comes not out of man's cunning thoughts,
but almost in spite of them.

God is not a conscious invention of a few clever men to
induce their followers to be good.

The belief in Him is all men's unconscious expression of their
deepest feelings about their world.

Man confronts the universe and cries out, "God!"

Almost as far back as we find any record of man—certainly as far back as he even dimly resembles man as we know him today— the records read that man was religious.

From his beginning, man was using magic or religious rites to have an ample supply of offspring, to have an ample supply of food, and to bury his dead.

The medicine man and the spell are as old as man. We find them painted on the walls of his oldest caves.

Man has thought of the powers that he looks to for help as outside himself.

He has thought of them as inside himself.

He has thought of them in religious terms.

He has thought of them in non-religious terms.

He has used rites, spells, propitiations, and sacrifices.

He has fasted and practiced sexual continence.

He has eaten sacred foods and smeared himself with unguents and ointments. He has sprinkled and dunked himself in holy waters.

He has taken drinks, drugs, and magic potions.

He has sung songs and danced dances.

He has used hypnotism and psychotherapy—in the name of Jehovah and in the name of Freud.

He has invoked spirits—of the gods and of the dead—and entered into trances.

All these things he has done—in the name of magic and of religion and of science—to touch and master for himself the powers beyond himself that he feels are there.

Everything he now does in scientific terms he has done in religious terms. Medicine, psychotherapy, the care of the crops, preparation for the hunt or for war, the maintenance and prosperity of the family and the nation—they were all once the province of the priest. It is no accident that alcoholic liquors are called spirits; they once were thought to be—as now some men hope LSD will be—an easy road to heaven.

But whether man is concocting new drugs (often the old potions of ancient religions, with new scientific names) or falling on his knees before an altar, he is only trying to make the breakthrough to powers beyond his own—to more love, more life, more intelligence, more power.

And man is right in feeling that there is power beyond any he has tapped—power within and outer power.

Man lives in seas of power. Crudely, primitively—with his dynamos and batteries and atomic piles—he draws off a little of the power without.

As to the power within, this he has handled even less effectively.

He is like a little crab who lives in a shallow tidal pool beside the sea.

He is very small and the sea is very large, and so he splashes in his little pool—but he knows that the sea is there; and the sea is his native element.

◦§ A *power beyond his own* §◦

It is this that man feels—and he feels it deeply—that there is a power beyond his own.

I wonder if there has ever been a man who has not felt this.

A sense of power! Incredible, almost inconceivable power; power to perform beyond anything he has ever done—or perhaps even dreamed of doing—a sense of power untouched, of capacities never put to work.

Man is right in feeling this. The power is there.

There is a larger power that he is capable of touching. There is a larger life that he is capable of living. He is meant for more—meant to do more, meant to be more.

What is man?

Whatever your answer, man is something more.

For man is that creation of God that must always be striving to be something more than what he has become.

So however he defines himself, whatever he thinks himself to be, he is that—and something more, something he has not yet grown to be, something he has not yet achieved or felt or thought or envisioned.

Because God made him in His image.

This is the image of the Infinite—and in man's finite form, the Infinite can be conceived of only in terms of something more.

Man looks up. The worlds of space wheel thundering over him. Man looks in. The tides of spirit tug at his soul. Around, within him are powers he feels he ought to harness, powers he feels he ought to realize.

He does not know how to lay hold of them. But he senses that he should. He senses that they are meant to be used and directed.

He lives on the surface of things—but beyond lies the deep, only waiting for him to dip the nets of his mind into its mysteries.

Beyond the shallow pool of self lies the deep sea of the More-than-self out of which man comes and through which he exists.

It is always this power beyond the limitations he has settled for, this truth beyond the facts he has accepted, this More-than-self beyond the self he has attained—it is always this that man is seeking, whether he calls it God or scientific knowledge.

This seeking I call prayer.

✎§ No respecter of names §✎

God is no respecter of names, not even His own. He is used to being called many names, and He has answered to all of them. They are all one to Him. The belief of the believer is what is important to God, and He answers according to that belief.

If the believer believes Him to be Ialdabaoth, God answers as Ialdabaoth. If the believer believes He is Jesus, God answers as Jesus. God has answered millions of people who have called on Him as Siva and Indra and Krishna and Ahura Mazda and Baal and Ra Amon and Thoth and Avalokita and Omito Fo and Kali and Kwanyin; for these are all names that worshipers have given Him.

And He has answered just as freely to names like Mind and Wisdom Heart and Absolute Suchness and the Void and the One and the Abyss and Nothing; for these, too, are names He has been named.

When Moses asked Him what His name was, He answered in such terms that almost every translator of what He said has given a different value to what He said. According to the most widely accepted English version, He said, "I Am That I Am"—which is subject to considerable speculation as to just what He did mean.

The Bible usually has a footnote to the effect that this might mean "I am what I am," or "I am because I am," or even, "I will be what I will be"—which He certainly will.

God, of course, spoke to Moses in Hebrew—not because that is God's native tongue but because it was Moses'. He knew that if He wanted Moses to understand, He had to speak in that tongue. God always speaks to everyone in the tongue he understands— Avestan to Zoroaster, Pali to the Buddha, Chinese to Confucius, Arabic to Mohammed, and English to me.

Sometimes, when He does not seem to care whether His listeners understand or not, He speaks to them in unknown tongues. Those who hear the unknown tongue seem to get spiritual excitement out of it; although they cannot tell us what they heard, they come away convinced that they heard God.

When God spoke to Moses—they had several conversations— Moses was so frightened and unsure of himself that he may not have given us a very exact account of the encounter. He was not even certain as to whether he saw God coming or going, let alone as to what God said to him.

Still Moses came off very well. He brought us back knowledge about God and our relationship with Him that has inspired and blessed us ever since.

◦§ Person or principle §◦

Perhaps the Easterners have the most to say about what God is —and this is because they say the least. They say that all that can be said about Him is, "He is."

The names that can be given—Him or anything else—are never absolute names.

The names we give anything are not ultimate names; they are just what we call it according to our latest viewpoint. Yesterday we called it something else, and tomorrow we will call it something else again. This goes for God and everything there is.

The earth, for instance, is round today, but it was flat yesterday and tomorrow it will be a hypersphere or whatever tomorrow's people see their world as being.

So it is with God.

He was a person yesterday, and still is for many.

But more and more people are coming to believe that what runs the world—and whether you give it lip service or not, what you believe really runs the world is your God—more and more people are coming to believe that this is Law.

We may take our children to church on Sunday; but when we depend on the doctor and the engineer to get us through all the other days of the week and provide us with our way of life, we are proclaiming—in spite of our protestations that we are a Catholic or a Baptist or a Seventh Day Adventist—that we believe that Law, not a Person, runs the world and we look to it to solve our problems.

Area after area of life, we are discovering, is run not by the changing fiats of a super-being, but by Law. Or laws. God is used to being thought of in the plural, too. Even the most fundamental name for Him in the Old Testament, Elohim, means "the gods."

ᵛᵉᵍ Savage and scientist ᵇᵉᵛ

God is—as the Hindus say. But God reveals Himself to us in the way He has to reveal Himself in order for us to understand Him at the level of understanding we have come up to.

Obviously savages are not going to get much help out of a God that is law—or abstract principles. Suppose God says to a savage: "I am the abstract principles best expressed in complicated mathematical formulas, which treat of the mechanical aspects or relatives of heat."

The savage is just going to look blank.

Likewise, suppose God says to a scientist: "I am Jehovah (or some other super-person) and I am in charge of the world. I let the sun come up and the moon go down. And I change things at my will. The best way for you to have a good life is for you to fall on your knees and beg me to be merciful."

The scientist just looks blank.

Now, do not misunderstand. The scientist no more has hold of the absolute name for God than the savage had. God is infinite and He is infinitely more than savages or scientists may tell you.

God is.

The notion that God is law is no more sacrosanct than that God is a person. And it is no more everlasting.

God is that which is real—and that which is realest about everything.

God is that which makes and runs the world.

Beyond making statements like these, there may not be much we can say about Him. And these statements clearly do not say much.

We can imagine the real. We can experience the real. But say much about it we cannot. Except, as I say, in relative terms.

You have to talk about the real in terms that make it meaningful to you—in terms of Jehovah, if that is what seems realest; in terms of thermodynamics and electromagnetics, if that is what seems realest.

God does not object to being thought of as the laws that govern the universe or the laws that govern human behavior. For such He is.

Only He is yet more.

And so is man.

Whatever man may think at the moment, he will not long settle for so little.

For man, like God, is more than a set of laws and reactions. This is not a physical universe governed by physical laws. This is a spiritual universe governed by spiritual yearnings. And man is a spiritual being.

If he tries to settle for less, he will find that he cannot. Man may leave God alone, but God will not leave man alone.

God will not let man be. He will prod him and press him and prick him and drive him.

If man will not swim out into the deep, God will hurl him out into the deep. God will hold him under the water until he has to swim.

God will stop at nothing to get man to become what He created man to be. God knows how much He may expect of man; He knows what man is capable of. So God insists that man reach beyond himself, for He made man to reach beyond himself. He made man always to seek to be something more.

Whatever you name the real, someone else—I hope this does not disturb you too much—is going to come along sooner or later, and show that this is not what it is; it is something more. Because mankind is not standing still. Man refuses to stop his unfoldment at the level you happen at present to have reached. Man is growing—and his understanding of what is real is growing with him.

I am sorry if this idea upsets you. If you happen to be powerful enough and well-enough organized, you may by authority and intimidation and murder arrest the growth of man's ideas for a few hundred years. But sooner or later, your children or grandchildren or great-grandchildren are going to run off and leave you and your idea. And sooner or later you are going to tag along after them. And the names you have named reality will decorate the museums and the history books of the new generation.

Heaven help the human race if this were not the case!

✑ The full turn of the wheel ໒∾

In our time, we see the proliferation of personality development courses—which are intended to do what we once did by falling on our knees and lighting a candle and dropping a penny in the offering box.

That is, they are intended to cure our illness, and postpone our death, and find us a job, and make us rich, and give us the husband or wife we want or get rid of the husband or wife we do not want, and enable us to gain the ascendancy over our friends and neighbors—in short, they are intended to enable us to become the very best person we are capable of being.

Today we talk about motivational research and personality development, and we use such methods as hypnosis and group therapy and psychoanalysis, if we have gone the full turn of the wheel and are altogether secular-minded; or, if we are still religious-minded, we talk of meditative methods of prayer, of affirmation and denial, of sitting in the silence, of unifying ourselves with the unitary-world-ground, and so on.

So, as I say, at this moment of history more and more people are coming to believe that life is controlled by law or laws.

Therefore it does no good for us who believe life is controlled by laws to fall on our knees and beg Mumbo Jumbo to help us. Instead, we have to learn these laws and apply them to life.

There are all kinds of laws. There are physical laws that heat and cool our homes and will shortly enable us to fly to the moon and back.

There are, also, mental laws that enable us to be happier and more successful and get along better in the human community—to win friends and influence people.

So we had best set about learning these laws.

Thus, in our time, prayer becomes more meditation than prayer. This, of course, it has always been among mystics, East and West.

Prayer becomes a process, not of appealing to a divine being, but of modifying our own psychological processes.

This is as it should be. Certainly, few would claim that God needs prayers; it is obviously man who needs them.

So it is right to think of prayer as changing man instead of changing God.

The moment we do this, we come up with methods of prayer that are designed to change our thinking.

The furthest out of our most completely non-religious youth have turned to using LSD and marijuana and glue and anything else that may possibly help them to expand their consciousness and pierce to a higher reality.

These would be the last persons in the world to say that they were seeking God.

But almost all primitive people have sought for God via sacred mushrooms and peyote and hashish and opium and soma and haoma—and—yes—even alcohol.

The identification of God and wine is much more ancient than the mass.

The terms change, but the methods remain the same. As I say, God chuckles at terms.

✑ Religion as a science ✒

It is interesting to note that the new religions that have grown up since man became science-minded think of themselves more as science than religion and often call themselves Christian Science, and Religious Science, and Divine Science, and Science of Mind, and Science of Being. The methods of prayer they have worked out are all methods that a scientific-minded person can believe in—and therefore methods that will work for such a person.

For a great teacher said long ago, "Whatsoever you believe in, this is what you will have."

They are all methods that presuppose that what we are working with is law or laws, and that a knowledge of these laws and the application of this knowledge to ourselves and our world will change us and our world.

Man, of course, is doing just this—finding laws and applying them—and finding that it works.

He is healing himself.

He is prospering himself.

He is winning friends and influencing people.

He is achieving goals.

And he is finding inner peace and integration, too.

If he calls himself an atheist, it is because he feels that he is working not with God but with principle.

God, of course, answers when He is called in the name of principle just as He answers when He is called in the name of the Lord Jehovah or the Lord Jesus—so long as you call, believing.

You cannot really believe in your inmost core that the world is run by scientific principles or laws, and get much of an answer when you call on a super-person. For your call on the super-person is going to be halfhearted. Where your faith is, that is where your real call will be directed.

In our time, few of us are altogether free of a belief in a super-person as running things and few of us are altogether free of a belief in scientific principle as running things.

So, prayer for most of us is becoming a mixture. There are elements of petition, elements of addressing a super-being; but more and more, elements of working with our own thinking, techniques like affirmation and denial, are appearing in our prayers.

Even the great orthodoxies, centuries old, are beginning to talk about affirmative methods of prayer, of silent sitting and listening—and the psychologist is invited into the church and occupies the little room alongside the confessional or the minister's study—or even, in more and more instances, occupies the confessional or study itself. For the minister and priest has become the psychologist.

And is this not necessary and desirable?

Man has always believed in the miracle workers. He is by nature a pragmatist. That is, he believes whatever works is true, and if anything is true, it works.

And man's faith is sound.

He is right to follow the miracle-workers. They are on the track. They are pointing the direction he has to go.

∽§ Science as a religion ξ∾

In our day, is there any question who the miracle-workers are? They are the scientists.

The scientists heal sickness.

They feed the hungry.

They bring water to the thirsty.

They prolong life.

They enable man to see what is going on 100,000,000 miles out in space.

They enable man to fly farther and higher than any bird.

They warm him in winter and cool him in summer.

They fill his life with color and music.

They free him from unpleasant tasks.

They give him powers he never dreamed of.

They even hint of personal immortality.

These are the miracle-workers and therefore these are now the new priests.

You may not think so, but ask yourself: Whom do you really look to as knowing the truth—about you or about your world?

Your minister? The Bible?

Or your doctor? Or the chemistry textbook?

If you are under twenty-five, there is no doubt as to how most of you will answer this question.

The scientists have not yet fully accepted this role as priests;

probably the priests did not accept it, at first. But they are on the way—and so are we.

The scientists, of course, are only beginning to discover what the laws are. In man's inner world, they have perhaps discovered no laws at all yet. Certainly, they are only beginning to work out methods of applying the laws to bring the results men want.

But today priests are becoming scientists, and scientists are becoming priests.

We look to them to tell us what is really the truth about ourselves and our world and we look to them to show us how to get what we want from life.

We are moving into a world where law is God and God is law. In this world religion is often going to assume a form that the people of a thousand years ago would have damned as an evil heresy. But the true religion of every new culture believes that the true religion of the preceding culture was a superstition.

Do you believe in Dionysus or Zeus or Indra or Thor or Osiris? False gods all, were they not? And the people who worshiped them were pagans and idolaters—is this not so?

So it is also with prayer.

The methods that our grandfathers used, we have begun to doubt will produce results.

In a world that is run by scientific principle—by law—we must come up with a science of prayer.

⤚ We are not yet there ⤙

We are not yet there. And perhaps the scientists will be wiser than the priests were, and not systematize the truth so rigidly, though scientists seem to be by their nature systematizers. But we can hope they will be wise.

The priests had hold of truth, and they did great things with the truth they had. Now the scientists have hold of truth, and they are doing great things. The priests had hold of part of the truth, and the scientists have hold of part of the truth; only they both insist on acting as if they had it all.

They spell out what truth is—and even more dangerously they spell out what it is not.

One day the devil was walking with a friend when they saw a man bend down and pick up something bright and shiny. The man looked around, saw that no one was watching, and hid what he had found in his pocket.

"What was that he found?" the devil's friend asked.

"He found a truth," said the devil.

"That's bad for you, isn't it?" said the friend.

"Not at all," said the devil. "I'm going to help him organize it."

When the Church began, into it came the brightest young people of the time—just as the brightest young people of our time want to be scientists. But they organized the truth they had. Instead of making man free, truth, when it was organized, bound them; instead of bringing them toward the light, it kept them in darkness.

If the scientists can just say to one another and the rest of us, "We have found some truth, but there is a lot more truth to be found. There are even truths that run counter to the truths we hold most dear," then there is hope. This, however, is not easy for anybody—least of all for those who have power and prestige and whom people look to as sages and authorities.

Nevertheless, a notion, even though it is held by very powerful and prestigious people, does not last forever.

There will always be heretics. The Grand Inquisitors of Science will be extremely skillful and hard to avoid, as Orwell and Huxley have already pointed out. But some men will manage.

Truth is hard to mummify. It has a way of rising even out of temples and museums. There will always be a Galileo muttering, as he stumbles out of the heresy trial, "But it still moves!" Or shouting it out as the flames—or whatever the twenty-second century equivalent of flames may be—begin to take effect.

It is not so much that old truths die as that new truths are born. Truth is alive and grows. It can no more stand still than life can stand still. Whatever you may say of it, tomorrow you will have to say something more. For it will be something more. Sometimes truths may get spoken before their time and vanish and have to be spoken again. But truths will always find someone to utter them. Sometimes they will be whispered or muttered or written down in secret books to be slipped surreptitiously from perilous hand to hand. Sometimes they will have to be taught in the caves and catacombs.

But they find utterance. Because those who would restrain and limit and fix them do not stand still, either. They, too, are alive and grow. Sooner or later the truths they are delivering in their incantations and their texts become less meaningful to them.

They continue to chant them and write them down in the sacred formulas. But they, too, begin to wonder.

Man is better for the religion he has had in the last five thousand years, whatever some cynics may believe. He will be better for the religion he will have in the next five thousand.

Man is coming always into a larger and grander concept of God, not, as I have said, because God changes, but because man is changing.

And he comes, also into larger and grander concepts of how to touch reality and how to make the good life.

III

WHERE DO I FIND GOD

❧ *I went out under heaven* ❧

I went out under the emptiness of heaven, and I could not find the Master. I cried to the heavens, "How shall I find him whom my soul loveth?"

The heavens replied, "You shall seek Him and find Him when you shall search for Him with all your heart."

I cried to the heavens, "Is this so?"

The heavens replied, "So it is with me. I give myself to those who give themselves to me. If you would know me, you must come to me night after night.

"You must give your life to me.

"You must give your mind to thoughts of me, burning to know, and you must give your heart to hopes of me, yearning to find.

"You must give me your waking hours and I must be what you dream about. You will wake for dreams of me, and fall asleep worn out with thinking of me.

"You must seek me with telescopes and observatories and theories, spectroscopes and radar antennae.

"You must glue your eyes to tubes that you have fastened on me until your eyes are leaden and burning from gazing at my wastelands and wonders and yet you cannot turn away.

"You must love me. For I give myself to none but my lovers.

"And I shall demand of you as a jealous mistress demands, 'Do you love me with all your heart? Is there none but me?'

"Then you must answer, 'Yes, with all my heart. There is none but you.'

"Then only shall I give myself to you.

"But then, indeed, you will not have to ask nor will I have to answer. You will know that you have given your heart to me and you will know that I have given my heart to you.

"I shall have revealed myself to you—my mysteries, my terrors, and my beauties, my apparent nature and my unknown soul—as much as you can bear to understand."

Then I saw that this was true. If I wanted to understand the heavens, I would have to give the heavens all my heart. If I wanted to understand any thing, I would have to give that thing all my heart.

I saw that so it is with everything.

Everything began to speak to me.

The earth, the waters of the earth, green growing things, creeping things, flying things, rocks, dust, mountains, particles too small for me to see.

All spoke, and all in the same voice.

I saw that if I would understand the boundless sea and know what deeps are like, I would have to give the sea all my heart.

If I would find the meaning of the small garden acre where I live, I must give this acre all my heart.

If I would find out what a speck of dust is, I must fall in love with it and pursue it with all the powers of my being, with heart and mind and might—and then, only then, would it open its heart to me and disclose its secret and essential meaning.

Whatever I give myself to, gives itself to me.

But, if this is true, the converse is also true.

Let me look at what I have, and I shall see what I have given myself to!

What do you have?

To this you have given your heart.

Look at your life, and you will see what you have been searching for—with all your heart and with all your soul and with all your might.

The lives of most of us are made up of nothing much, because we do not give all our heart and soul to anything. We give a dribble here and a dab there, and we get a drab dribble-dab back.

We have a little prosperity, a little lack, a little health, a little ill-health, a little happiness, a little unhappiness.

We drink a little stale wine left as dregs in the cup when we could drink from the casks of the gods.

Let us fall in love with life.

Let us give ourselves to living.

Let us search with all our heart for Him we love.

For when we search with all our heart, we shall seek and find Him.

✥ You have a compass ✥

Then I asked, "How do I seek with all my heart?"

The answer came:

You must seek in your times of prayer. You must also seek in times when you do not pray.

When you sit down to pray, you cry out, "God! God!" and you feel that you are seeking, that you have turned your heart to Him and are yearning after Him.

But you sit down to pray only a few minutes every day. Perhaps many days you take no time to pray at all.

What are you seeking then?

If you seek God for five minutes a day, fifteen minutes a day, an hour a day, even four hours a day, what is your heart seeking? What is your heart seeking when it is not turned to God? What is your heart seeking when, undisciplined by thoughts of prayer, it roams around your daily world? Tasting this, trying that, it goes, giving itself to the delights of curiosity and to curious delights, experimenting here, experiencing there, pursuing pleasure, evading pain.

We put our mind and heart and hands to many different pursuits, some worthwhile, some not worthwhile.

In order to live we have to spend time earning a living, studying, playing, sharing with family and friends, meeting the needs of our body, being part of a community.

If to live we must seek all these things, how then shall we seek God with all our heart?

There is only one way.

We have to put God into all we seek.

I have to seek a living. But I can work for God in my work.

I have to care for my friends. But I can care for God in my friendships.

I have to give myself freely to play. But I can see God in the light side of life, no less in play than in work—and this will help me to see God everywhere in the world.

I have to be part of my community. But I can make God part of my community and make my community God's.

Wherever you turn, God is there. Search for Him, then, in all that you do.

God is that magnetic pole to which the compass of the heart is tuned. By keeping yourself pointed to Him, you find all the directions in your life.

When you have no truth to which your heart must turn and when it turns away must turn again, how shall you ever know where you are? Or where you are going?

Even if your life is filled with the luckiest of incidents, they are always merely incidents—passing, meaningless, because they take you nowhere—or even if they do take you somewhere, you cannot know where they are taking you. Though you drift from summer sea to summer sea of pleasure, nevertheless you drift.

God is a sense of spiritual direction.

Without God to center yourself in, though you chance to find yourself in Paradise, you have no meaning or direction. You are still happenstance in a world of happenstance.

Once you point your thought toward God—even though you may find yourself in hell—you know which way you have to go.

You have a sense of spiritual direction, a sense of destination. You are not lost; you can chart your way.

Even in an unknown world you can know whether you merely wander in lost circles of frustration or whether you are going in a straight line of faith.

⋐ Of refuse heaps and mountaintops ⋑

God is the truth by which you measure all thoughts to see how true they are.

God is the love by which you measure all acts to see how good they are.

God is the joy by which you measure all events to see how full they are.

God is that in all you are doing by which you judge its worth, for God is the good end and purpose of all you are doing.

God is in everything, or He is in nothing. If you can find Him anywhere, you can find Him in all that you encounter.

He is in your pleasure and in your pain, in your kind and cruel acts, in conditions that satisfy and conditions that horrify you.

God is as much in the darkness as in the light, as much in shame as in glory, as much in the ugly as in the beautiful, as much in the ramblings of the demented as in the inspired speech of the poet, as much in the absurd as in the rational.

Have great inventions, great discoveries of truth, great acts of love, great works of inspiration come out of times of prayer, out of the calm contemplation of the beautiful? They have come much more out of active engagement in life and troubled consideration of painful events.

Beautiful flowers blossom not only in sheltered gardens, but in drab ditches and out of refuse heaps.

Human greatness comes as often out of slums and tenements as out of palaces. Human greatness springs most often of all out of great challenges and great needs.

Strength comes as a response to burdens to bear. Intelligence is our response to problems to solve. Love is our answer to loneliness and pain.

Zoroaster said that he sought God because he heard "the wail of the kine"; the Buddha, because he became aware of the extent of human suffering.

Do not look for God to be only in happy times, only in pleasant happenings.

Do not look for good to be only in good people or truth to be only in sincere people. Love dwells in unlovely hearts and light in darkened minds.

When we search with all our heart, God cries out to us from the refuse heap as from the mountaintop, "You shall seek me and find me when you shall search for me with all your heart."

God is the good. The good is God. To search for God with all our heart is to search for the good with all our heart. We have to look for the good. We have to long for the good. We have to set our heart toward the good. We have to call forth the good.

And the good—what is this?

Surely the good is whatever makes for life. It is love, intelligence, order, energy—whatever form these may take.

We shall find God when we shall take Him into our activity as well as our times of contemplation. We shall find God when we make Him a constant companion, not a sometime thing that we encounter only in prayer or worship.

Life becomes prayer and worship when we look for God in all we encounter.

The earth is our cathedral, life is our liturgy, time is the rosary whose beads we tell—when we look for the good even in the evil event, even in the evil intent.

All life becomes a song of praise when we delight in its events.

All life becomes a hymn of faith when we search out its meaning.

Can I find the good in a drug addict?

Can I find the good in a murderer?

My shame and yours—the secret deed, the hidden, furtive thought—shall we think to hide these from Infinite Intelligence —or shall we cry out, "Even here, God, even here," and feel the healing touch of Love!

I look at men and I see their infinite potential for evil—I see them rob and lie and cheat and torture—I see them degrade themselves and others.

Yet I look at men and see their infinite potential. The depth to which they sometimes fall shows me the height to which they sometimes rise.

Even man's depths—what an abyss of hope and terror!

It is no accident that hell is thought of as bottomless—hell is man's assessment of his own capacity for pain. But if I make my bed in hell, shall I not look for God there?

⋞§ To pray without ceasing §⋟

We search for God with all our heart when we pray without ceasing. We pray without ceasing when we look for the good in all we encounter and try to draw it forth.

To pray without ceasing does not mean that we constantly

think about God or that we keep the word, "God! God!" on our lips.

We pray without ceasing when we habitually meet whatever comes to us with faith and with love, with a mind to draw from the event all that it has to give, with a willingness to do whatever has to be done to make the most and the best of it.

We pray without ceasing when we refer the events of life to God.

We do this not so much by having times to pray—though we need these—as by acting all the time, as much as we are able, with courage, faith, love, power, and intelligence. We do this not so much by speaking words as by our inward attitude.

To pray without ceasing is to keep our heart attuned to what God means in life.

God is. Infinite, perfect, absolute. Beyond all that we can say of Him.

But in the life of human beings, he is those human qualities divine which are most God-like.

He is faith.

He is courage.

He is love.

He is intelligence.

He is energy.

He is order.

Faith may be falling on our knees, but it is more likely to be standing firm or walking on. It may be waiting. It may be working. It may be daring to step out on uneasy waters. It may be just daring to step out.

Courage may be making courageous affirmations about life, but it is more likely to be going forward when we would rather have gone back. Courage may be standing still when we would rather have run away. Courage may be running away when we would rather have stood firm.

Love may be throwing ourselves at the feet of the Lord devotedly, but love may also be giving a gift we would rather have kept for ourselves. Love may be speaking a longed-for word. Love may be withholding a word we should not speak. Love may be binding up wounds, sometimes wounds we cause. Love may be setting someone free—sometimes someone we would like to bind to us. Love may be putting another's good ahead of our own. Love may be feeling how others feel. Love may be living with others and living for others.

Intelligence may be thinking about God. But intelligence may just be thinking clearly. Intelligence may be quiet listening. Intelligence may be original insight. Intelligence may be seeing through facts to the truth.

Laughter may be prayer. So may tears.

To shoulder a heavy load with a light heart is to meet things with God. To be deeply moved by the need of another human being, by noble action, by beauty, or truth—this is to be aware of God.

Standing still may be a prayer. So, too, may action.

One of the highest forms of prayer is work. Give yourself to a creative purpose. Let your mind and hands be absorbed in bringing forth some good thing—a field of wheat, or a poem, or a machine—and you draw very close to God.

God is the creative Spirit. When you give yourself to the working of that Spirit, you are one with God.

To pray without ceasing is to put God in charge of your life. It is to look for direction. It is to expect inspiration.

It is to feel that you are serving the ends and purposes of life more than your own ends, and to make your own ends—as much as you can—life's ends.

It is, in a sense, to have one prayer always in your mind: "Here am I, God—Life, Love, Mankind—use me."

IV

TEACH ME TO PRAY

✑ *I heard the whole world praying* ܀

I said to the Master, "Teach me to pray."

The Master said, "What prayer would you have me teach you?"

He caught me by the hand and carried me to the top of the world. All the prayers of the world rise there.

Then I heard the whole world praying.

I heard little children on their knees beside their beds. I heard monks at their morning prayers. I heard nuns telling beads. I heard Hail Marys and Our Fathers and all the prayers in the Book of Common Prayer.

I heard the people of Japan and China whispering before their Buddha shelf, over and over and over, "Namo Omito Fo! Hail Amida Buddha!" I saw that there were some who prayed this prayer with every breath they drew, and they had prayed in this manner for years.

Like the everlasting thunder of sea surf the roar of the *shahada* rolled continually from millions of Moslem throats: "La ilaha illa Allah: Muhammadun rasul'allah." There is no God but God, and Mohammed is his messenger! At sunrise, at noon, in midafternoon, at sunset, at darkfall, day in, day out, I watched the whole world of Islam prostrate itself and pour out prayers to Allah.

I smelt the sandalwood fires of the Parsees that burn continually in the Fire-temples, and I saw the Parsees on their knees at their rites of penance and cleansing and blessing.

I heard the clatter and whirl of uncounted prayer wheels turning forever in the mountain cities of Tibet. I saw the prayer banners flapping and straining in the winds of faith. *Om Mani Padme Hum.* Aum! The Jewel in the Lotus! Aum!

In the Zen monasteries I saw the rows of young men, poised,

silent, intent, juggling morning and evening the koan of nothingness, straining with all their power of thought to think what
thought cannot.

I saw the yogins sitting for years in the lotus posture, seeking
moksha and *samadhi,* release and blessedness. I felt their thoughts
drawn forth in straight, thin, unbroken lines to link them with
the object of their thoughts.

I saw dervishes whirling in their frenzied dances, piercing themselves with knives and spears.

I saw masked witch doctors howling and leaping through their
throbbing rites.

I saw the Pope making the sign of the Cross over the multitudes
in the Square of St. Peter's.

I saw centuries of Chinese emperors mounting the stairs of the
Temple of Heaven, carrying gifts of silk and incense and wine to
celebrate the reborn sun.

I saw over all the endless earth the endless, senseless sacrifice
turning temples into butchershops, and I smelt its reek.

From countless Jewish homes, I heard the age-old chant:
"Shema Yizroel Adonai Elohenu Adonai Echod." Hear, O Israel,
the Lord our God is one Lord!

I heard men reciting prayers in languages they had forgotten,
and men speaking tongues they could not understand.

I heard lamentations and praises and petitions, and I heard
the sound of silence. I heard drums and bells and whistles, and
I heard the sound of every musical instrument ever invented.

I heard the cries of those who believed in many gods and
saints. I heard the thoughts of those who did not believe in God
at all, but believed in the power of thought.

I heard spells that had been spun before the memory of man.
I heard men coax and wheedle. I heard them threaten and
demand. I watched them act out their wish before their god.

I heard selfless prayers. I heard selfish prayers. I heard men
pray for their enemies to be destroyed. I heard men pray for
their enemies to be blessed. I heard men pray for themselves. I
heard men pray for others.

I saw priests perform many-splendored rites that took years to
complete. I saw prayers that were hardly a moment's thought.

I saw men whipping themselves with whips until they bled.

I saw men crouching all their lives on pillars. I saw men living all their lives in caves. I saw men spending all their lives disciplining their mind so that they could think the thought they wanted to think. I saw men spending all their lives disciplining their mind so that they could think no thought at all.

I saw men performing every conceivable act—murdering, mutilating themselves and others, practicing every kind of sexual act, taking drugs, drinking, gambling, fasting, devouring every kind of food and drink, even one another—and all these men, I could see, considered themselves to be praying.

I saw men giving freely of their wealth and going out of their way to help those who were less fortunate and even giving up their life—and these men, too, were praying.

I heard all the names of all the gods invoked in these prayers; there would not be room in this book to write down all these names.

All these prayers arose like smoke—thought and feeling and desire flowing together, incense and bells and flame, ritual and robe and mask, motions of dancers and fixed immobility, shouting and wailing and singing and silence and endless repetitions—all steaming upward in a vast welter of sights and sounds and smells.

Then the Master said again, "What prayer would you like me to teach you?"

Then in that hubbub, suddenly I felt every man reaching out of himself and into himself to be more than he had been before he prayed; and I knew that every man must pray at the level of his own experience and out of his own nature; and that I had to pray because of what I am and from where I am, out of my own desire and by my own belief.

Then I said, "Teach me the prayer that is my own to make."

❧ An infinity of roads ☙

There is not one best way of prayer for all people.
Every man has to pray at the level of his own awareness.
What is your level of awareness?
What do you believe you are?
What do you believe God is?

What do you believe is the relationship that exists between you?

If I believe I have to swim across a river, I will prepare in a different way than if I believe I can wade across it, or if I believe I can cross on a bridge or a ferryboat, or if I believe the river is a mirage.

And perhaps the river is all these things. It depends on where we stand along the bank.

You and all men pray to contact a higher power than you ordinarily have contact with.

This power may seem to be outside you—and you may call it God or gods. You may give it many names.

This power may seem to be inside you—and you may call it your Higher Self or your subconscious or superconscious or God in you. You may give it many names.

You may think of it as a person.

You may think of it as a principle.

It makes no difference to the power what name you call it. Reality is no respecter of names. It answers to the name you name.

But it makes a great deal of difference to you what name you call it.

The name you give the power—the way you see the power—will determine the way you pray.

Is one way of prayer better than another way?

Is it better to build straw houses, or glass houses, or skyscrapers?

Is it better to be a poet, a scientist, a farmer, or a priest?

Is it better to raise wheat, to manufacture automobiles, to work problems in mathematics, or to write a book on prayer?

God is infinite.

Does it seem likely that there is only one road to the Infinite? There must be an infinity of roads, however long and roundabout some of them may be.

Some men like to feel that they alone of all men have found the way to God or have the right to approach Him, but how small the god must be who has only one way to Him.

Even a tiny oasis in a desert has more than one way to it. And in what direction can you go and not reach the ocean?

God is more everywhere at hand at the same time than the ocean is.

The way to pray is the way that makes God real to you.

For there is a power.

There is a presence.

There is a Something.

If you have not experienced it, what words will make it real to you? If you have experienced it, what words will you need?

We may encounter this Something anywhere at any time.

It may come as the lightning and as a thief in the night. It may also come slowly. It may come quietly, naturally, as naturally as waking after sound sleep, as naturally as seeing the sun rise in the morning.

Jacob wrestled with an angel at the ford Jabbok.

Paul encountered reality on the road to Damascus.

But for most of us, the ford Jabbok and the road to Damascus are in our own mind. It is there our angel lurks, and it is there we wrestle with the things of Spirit.

It is with our own thoughts we contend and in our own nature we come face to face with God, if we ever do.

Is God then Something in myself?

You may not think it is right to say that He is, but it is certainly not right to say He is not.

The tree is more than the tiny root tip that grubs unseen in the earth.

Yet the root tip can say, "The tree and I are one."

And I can say, "God and I are one."

Can an atheist pray?

All men pray, though they do not call it prayer.

For all men reach beyond themselves. All men try to be more than they have been. All men try to touch powers beyond those they ordinarily have access to.

Whenever men try to do this, they are praying.

You do not have to know God's name to have His help.

A man was lost in a wood. He wandered aimlessly until at last he came to a clearing. In the middle of the clearing was a house.

The man ran to the house and knocked at the door crying for help.

When the owner of the house, who was a kind and gentle person, came to the door and saw the man, bedraggled and frightened, he took him in and fed him.

He did not ask, "Do you know who I am? And have you called me by my right name?"

The man knocked at the door and the owner of the house took him in.

So it is with God.

When we come to God's house and knock in our need, He does not care whether we call Him by His right name; He does not care whether we are holy or unholy; He does not care whether we are believers or unbelievers.

God is love and His love shuts no one out.

And God's house has many doors.

The name of one is prayer.

The name of another is meditation.

The name of another is deep thought.

The name of another is selfless acts of faith.

Any time we go beyond self we come to selflessness, and another name for selflessness is God.

Any time we go beyond our own resources, we come to resources that are more than our own, and a name for these resources is God.

Any man who acts in love works in God, for God is a name for love as love is a name for God.

Do you listen, hopeful that there will come to you a whisper of truth no one has ever heard before?

Do you look, hopeful that there will break upon your sight some vision of perfection no one has ever seen before?

Do you seek, hopeful that you will find a way no one has happened on before?

Do you work, hopeful that you will produce something that will make the world a better place for you and your fellow men?

If you do any of these, you pray—perhaps a truer prayer than is his who repeats empty words in idleness.

The most spiritual man I ever knew called himself an atheist.

"Sometimes," he told me once, "when I read a great 'poem,

it is as if for a moment an edge of the veil is lifted and I see through to a reality beyond this world that we inhabit, but of a God I see no evidence."

The man was a doctor. He rose early. He went to bed late. Between those times he was continually seeking to heal the sick of mind and spirit and body. He took payment from those who could pay—and he lived richly—but he gave freely to those who could not pay.

If there is a time when we come face to face with God and know Him as He is, I can see this man standing before God then.

When God declares, "Let all who love Me come to Me," and the multitude of eager hopeful souls surge forward around His knees, this man will not go forward but will stand back, thinking, "I did not even believe in Him."

Then Love will whisper softly:

"But I was an hungered, and you gave me meat; I was thirsty, and you gave me drink; I was a stranger, and you took me in; I was naked, and you clothed me; I was sick, and you visited me; I was in prison, and you came to see me."

Then I can hear the man reply, "But Lord, I did not even believe in you. When saw I you an hungered, and fed you? or thirsty, and gave you drink? When saw I you a stranger, and took you in? Or naked, and clothed you? When saw I you sick or in prison, and came to you?"

And Love will answer, "Inasmuch as you have done it to one of the least of these my brethren, you have done it to me." And Love will go forward to embrace him.

For God is no respecter of words. They love Him who serve Him with words, but they love Him even more faithfully who serve him, not with words, but with attitudes and action.

Whoever serves love, whoever serves intelligence, whoever serves life—he serves God.

Whoever serves man, he serves God.

All you atheists who love your fellows and seek to relieve their sufferings and to make their world a better place in which to live, I tell you, you are no atheists—however, vigorously you may affirm your unbelief. You are true believers all.

All those who give themselves away to that which they feel to be of highest worth, though they have no faith or hope in an

Eternal Being, are more truly His faithful followers than those who throw themselves on their knees crying, "God, God," but give little of themselves away to life or to man.

When Love cries out, "Did you love Me?" who answers best? He who says, "I did not love man, but I believed in God," or he who says, "I did not believe in God, but I loved man."

A man named John once wrote in his Book, "If a man says, 'I love God,' while hating his brother, he is a liar," but "he who dwells in love is dwelling in God, and God in him."

⤳ *What are you asking for?* ⤲

We think of prayer as a brief encounter between us and God. Prayer is a time set aside when we speak to Him, usually asking for something we want, and he answers us—or does not answer us.

But all of life is an encounter between us and God. All the time we are speaking to God, asking something we want of Him; but even more, He is speaking to us, asking something He wants of us.

Prayer is a time of words but it is also a time of silence. Often at our encounter with God no words are spoken at all.

For we pray with our attitudes.

Generosity is a prayer.

So is grasping and clutching.

The prayer that is grasping and clutching has, of course, a different answer than the prayer that is generosity.

Courageously going forward to face what has to be faced is a prayer.

So is running away.

Keeping faith in the good in the face of all appearances to the contrary is a prayer.

So is failing to keep faith.

All these prayers, too, have different answers.

Our life shapes us, and we shape our life.

For we build our life a thought at a time—there is no other way.

Some moments of our life seem more crucial and important

than the others—but we reached these special moments by way of all the other moments; we reached them by taking steps in one direction rather than in another—and we took these steps one at a time.

What are you praying now?

For you are praying.

You are directing certain petitions to life as surely as you do when you enter a church and fall on your knees before an altar.

You are asking life to give you certain things and to keep certain things from you.

You are asking just as certainly and demandingly as if you were crying and importuning aloud.

What are you asking life for?

Are you saying, "Strike me! Hurt me! Humiliate me!"

Or are you saying, "Bless me! Enrich me! Lift me up!"

Are you saying, "Help me to avoid responsibility! Give me a way of not having so much to meet!"

Or are you saying, "Give me strength. Give me more to do. Help me to see if I cannot lift a heavier load."

Are you saying, "I see."

Or are you saying, "I am lost."

Are you saying, "Give to me."

Or are you saying, "Give through me."

Are you saying, "Give me work to do."

Or are you saying, "I don't like to work."

For you are saying these things. Yes, you may be saying all these things all at the same time.

Only some you say aloud and some silently, in your secret soul.

Some you cry out for everyone to hear and some for no one but God; you even try not to hear what you are saying yourself. Some you may even hope God will not hear—or at least will pay no attention to.

Some you admit that you say. Some you deny.

But life answers them all. And life grinds out its answers exceeding fine.

Life has a scales in which it weighs the cries of your heart. All that you give to it, life weighs on its scales. It balances this against that—and it pays you according to the balance.

If you bring life ignorance and fear, life pays you in pain and anxiety.

If you bring life knowledge and faith, life pays you in blessings and peace.

And if you bring life your will, saying, "Here is my will, I lay it down before you," it pays you by giving you life's will—and life's will is always yet more, yet more for you.

If you bring life your body and lay it down before life, life will lift it up and fill its veins with vigor and its limbs with strength.

If you bring life your mind and spread it out before life, life will fill it with knowledge and bless it with light.

If you bring life your life, life will make it one with Itself, and you will find that you have not just the little life you felt you had—to lose or keep—but you are one with all the life there is.

You are not a thread, but a rope. For in the rope of life an infinity of threads are so intricately woven together that no thread can say, "I am this and you are that," but every thread can only say, "I am the rope."

You are not a drop of water to be evaporated by any chance ray of sunlight; you are the sea. For in the sea of life, the drops are one. You have no ending or beginning; at your center, sea, and at your circumference, sea. You go to make up the sea. You flow out of sea and flow into sea again and you are never separate from the sea. The sea must say, "I am this drop," and you must say, "I am this sea."

You are not a spark flying upward from the hearth but you are the fire itself. For in the fire of life, where are the boundaries? Of what spark does the fire say, "I am not this spark"? And what spark shall say, "I am not this fire"? The fire cannot separate itself from you nor can you separate yourself from the fire. You can only say of yourself, "I am fire."

When you give your life to life, your life becomes one with all the life there is and you see that you neither began when you began nor will end when you end; but you come out of life and go into life. You cannot be separated from life, because your life is not a separate thing, but one with that which has always been and always will be.

You are not a thread but a rope.

You are not a drop but a sea.

You are not a spark but a conflagration.

You are not a little, separate, frightened, aching life, but one with all the life there ever has been or ever will be, out of life into life everlastingly moving.

⋖ Life is a wonder ⋗

Life is not a problem in arithmetic, adding one and one and arriving at lovely round sums. After you have added up all the numbers there are to add up, you still have an infinity left over. You are not going to learn to live life by learning a few simple rules and applying them—or a lot of complicated rules. You cannot measure life in meters or weigh it in grams, as physicists and chemists try to do. You cannot catch it in words and put it into a book, as philosophers and theologians try to do.

Life—this life—all the life we know about—begins with a birth and ends with a death. Beyond birth and death lies mystery. We may have dreams and visions and hints and hopes as to what is there, yet it remains mystery.

O blessed mystery, O fortunate us, that we do not have to live in eternity, but only in this little space in time.

We come into view and we pass out of view. In the interval between these incidents, much occurs. And even of this little interval, there is more that we do not understand than that we do understand.

Life is not a problem. Life is a wonder. Prayer, at its highest, is a recognition of the wonder and a hallelujah of delight that we are more than anything we can think we are and part of a world that is an everlasting succession of surprises.

V

HAS EAST OR WEST THE ANSWER

❦ *The East and the West of truth* ❧

I said to the Master,

"Where, then, will man find methods of prayer, ways of thought, that will help him most in this present age? Should we look to the East or the West for the better way to the truth?"

The Master said, "If I wish to circumnavigate the globe, shall I go to the East or to the West? Which side of a coin is the truer side?"

Then I saw how Western man has looked at his outside world. Eastern man has looked at his world inside. Western man has examined into the nature of things. Eastern man has examined into the nature of thoughts.

Western man, looking at things, has come up with a truth that is akin to thought. Eastern man, looking at thought, has come up with a truth that is akin to things.

To the West a truth is a statement you read in a book—preferably a science book—Boyle's law, or the Copernican Theory, or Heisenberg's principle of indeterminacy.

Go ask any of the great truth-finders of the West—you will find them in a research laboratory, will you not?—to give you a truth. Will he go out and pick you a flower?

Or will he open a book and read from it, "$e=mc^2$" or, "The square of the hypotenuse of a right triangle is equal to the sum of the squares of the other two sides"?

Ask yourself, dear Western reader, if this is not what you think a truth to be?

But ask an Eastern master for a truth. You will find him sitting cross-legged and still, contemplating his own true nature with such fixed unwavering intensity that at last he identifies with his own true nature—not thinking, "That One am I," but becoming that One.

If he answers you in words at all, he may say something like, "You are yourself the truth you seek."

Or he may ask you another question, such as, "What were you before you were born?"

Or he may just say, "Walk on."

The Buddha did not have a thought as he sat under the Bo-tree. He had an experience. He never was altogether successful in communicating to the rest of us just what he did experience.

He called it nirvana—but just what nirvana is is debatable to this day—to those who have not experienced it.

Not having entered it, you cannot conceive what it is.

Enter in, and you do not have to ask what it is.

Knowledge of truth to the East is akin to sensory experience.

It is like drinking water, and knowing that it quenches thirst.

It is like knowing what blue is.

If you are blind, how shall I ever make you know? If you are highly intelligent, your mind may grasp the intellectual concept of blue as a wave length of light. But this is a black-and-white blue.

Once you have experienced blue, I do not have even to speak the word "blue." I step with you under the noonday sky—and there it is!

⊸§ At each extreme its opposite §⊷

How strange that the West—to whom truth is an intellectual thing—cannot keep their mental hands off the world and are constantly changing it and tinkering with it.

Almost the only ideas they are interested in are ideas about the world.

But the East—to whom truth is not an intellectual thing—pay no attention to the world at all. They let it slide past them as if it were not there.

Almost the only experiences they value are experiences within themselves.

The yogin when he attains the essential truth about himself

realizes that his mind and his thoughts are as unreal and illusory
—as little part of truth—as everything else.

Trying to describe his experience of ultimate truth, he tells us
that it is like being a spectator seated high on a mountain cliff
watching far below him travelers passing on a road. The travelers
are his thoughts. The road is his mind. Detached and indifferent,
he is neither mind nor thought. Nor is truth mind or thought.

Somehow the view of East and West should be the other way
around. The West should not see truth as thought; the East
should see truth as thought.

The fact that it is the way it is makes me wonder what reality
—or God—really is like. I have a feeling we do not know; or—I
started to put down—we know only as a child in kindergarten
knows mathematics. But I stopped as I suddenly realized that such
a statement shows how brainwashed I am. Knowledge of reality,
naturally to a Westerner like me, is like knowledge of mathematical principles.

What is really real?

So often when we go to an extreme, instead of getting what
logic bids us expect, we get its opposite.

Reason followed far enough becomes unreasonable.

Unreason followed far enough becomes reasonable.

Often, when I see human beings affirming something very
loudly, I discover, if I can get into their heart and their way
of life, that what they are affirming there—in their heart and in
the way they live—is the opposite of what their tongues attest to.

O saints, what is your private nastiness? Ogres, what is the
happy virtue that is your secret shame?

The love of life may hide the fear of death, and spiritual
growth may be a pretty name for self-centeredness.

⋙ God has a sense of humor ⋘

Considering all this, I see once more that this is a world of
paradoxes, inconsistencies, and contradictions—and by that very
fact a world of sweet and perfect balance. And I hear once more
the gentle laughter I have caught from time to time on my
wanderings. Have you never heard life laughing? I do not mean

the bitter mocking some men seem to hear—the mockery of mean-
inglessness. It is, in fact, the very opposite—I have always felt
when I have heard this laughter that I have had an insight into
meaning and found it a merriment.

I have always felt, whatever made the world, it has to be a
happy spirit, for I have heard it laughing. I have heard reason
taking joy in the ridiculousness of the reasonable—and in the
reasonableness of the ridiculous. I have heard God chuckling at
the jest of justice.

Sometimes I feel that God must be a person—else why is there
a sense of humor at the heart of things? A principle with a sense
of humor—that is hard to believe! And there is a sense of
humor, make no mistake. Something that tosses a banana peel
under goose-stepping pomposity. Something that provides an un-
seemly, but how suitable, correction for any balloon that swells
itself beyond its seemly limits.

I do not mean that I really believe God to be a person. If he
is, I have to revise my notion of what a person is. For it almost
seems a kind of blasphemy to think of the Ultimate Reality as
something like myself, though it is easy to think of myself as being
like the Ultimate Reality.

You may have trouble seeing a difference, but that is because
you have a one-way look.

You are like the stewardess on the plane going from Washington to New York.

A man who had had too much to drink stopped her and asked:
"How long does it take to get from Washington to New York?"
"Twenty-eight minutes," she told him.

As she came back through the plane, the man stopped her again
and asked:

"How long does it take to get from New York to Washington?"
"I just told you, twenty-eight minutes," said the stewardess.
"No, you said, it took twenty-eight minutes to get from Washington to New York. Now I want to know how long it takes
to get from New York to Washington?"

"If it is twenty-eight minutes from Washington to New York,
it's twenty-eight minutes from New York to Washington."

"I don't know," said the man. "It's only a week from Christmas to New Year's; and look how long it is from New Year's to Christmas."

How far I often am from God, but how close God always is to me!

All I am saying here is that the Ultimate Reality seems as much like a person as it does like a law. It has aspects that make me want to say, Impersonal Principle. It has aspects that make me want to say, loving Father.

For if it has a sense of humor, it is not a cruel sense of humor, but a warm smile. It pokes a gentle fun at our absurdities and exaggerations, as a kind grandfather might at the swaggerings and exaggerations of his beloved grandson.

If Reality has a sense of humor, it has also a heart of compassion.

ᴥᥑ Thing-thoughts and thought-things ᢧᥐ

Perhaps the Chinese see the world most clearly of all of us when they see it as nothing fixed, but as made up of interacting energy modes, which they call yin and yang. Yin is passivity; yang is activity. These are continually turning one upon the other, so that at the height of yin, yang is beginning to emerge, and at the height of yang, yin is beginning to emerge. In the fullness of the perfection of yang, at its very core, there is always a seed of yin; in the fullness of the perfection of yin, there is always a taint of yang.

There is a great law that corrects excesses. And this it does not by forbidding them, but by constructing things in such a manner that when we go far enough in any direction we come out in the opposite direction.

No one should ever seek for truth except one who does not mind going in circles. For truths are always circles and turn back on themselves. When you find a straight-line truth, it only means that you have not looked far enough. You have a little piece of truth. If you follow a straight line far enough, it always curves back on itself; as a matter of fact, this is truer of straight lines than of any other kind.

So it is with East and West.

The Easterner, wanting to know the truth of bamboo, goes and sits in the bamboo grove. There he listens; there he watches; there he lives. He puts down roots with the bamboo; he puts forth stems and leaves; he himself grows one with earth and opens his heart to sun and rain. Until at last he cries out, "I am bamboo!"

The Westerner wanting to know the truth of bamboo consults a book about it. He sets up tables and mechanisms to analyze its growth and content. He records its history from seed to fodder. He sections and blueprints it. He learns everything there is to learn about it. Until he can say, "Bamboo is any of various woody or treelike grasses of the genus Bambusa or other related genera, as Arundinaria, Dendrocalamas."

In the West, the fact-finder reduces things to thoughts.

In the East, the thinker becomes the thing.

VI

GOD—PERSON OR PRINCIPLE

৺ঙ *God, are you there?* ৪৶

I said to the Master,
"Sometimes prayer is like a call, 'God, are you there?'"
The Master said,
"And sometimes I wonder if God does not send out an answering call, 'Man, are you there?'"

Man has come to a fork in the road.

He sees his world as a world of contradictions.

The old values molder, the old rules change, the old certainties crumble, but he is not yet sure of any new ones.

Shall he go this way or that?

Shall he turn here or there for help?

I do not believe there has ever been a thinking man who did not have times when he doubted that there is a God.

He looks at the world and he sees so much suffering and cruelty that it makes him question that love can be at work there—and if God is not Love, what is He?

He calls, "God, God!" but he hears no answering voice. He prays but nothing happens—or if it does, it is not anything that he can recognize as an answer to his prayer.

It is interesting that usually the more intelligent a man is, the harder time he has believing. It is easy to see why, of course—he sees all the reasons for not believing.

For this world is full of reasons for believing, but it is also full of reasons for not believing. When in our probing we pry out enough of the latter, no matter how many of the former we may find, we begin to doubt. Part of our reason for doubt is that we think of God as a person like ourself. When we talk to Him as a man, we expect Him to talk to us as a man. We expect to hear a soothing—or even an angry—voice, and we expect to feel a comforting arm around our shoulders—or a kick in the pants.

But God is not a man. God is not like a man. I may be like Him—in the essence of myself, whatever that is—but He is not like me. I get to thinking He is like me because He has to operate on the level where I am if I am to encounter Him—or recognize Him when I do.

If He does not speak to me in English, He cannot speak to me at all—because I will not understand what I hear.

If He cannot reveal Himself to me in some form I recognize as divine, He cannot appear to me at all—because I will not know Him when I see Him.

If I am convinced God is a person, He is going to have to look like a person, He is going to have to talk like a person, He is going to have to act like a person—or no matter what happens to me, I will not believe God had a hand in it.

None of us, no matter what we may say, actually in our heart altogether believe God is like this, but much of the time we cry after Him as if we do.

We are all like the boy starting to slide off the roof and calling out, "God! God, help me!" and a moment later adding, "It's all right, God. I don't need help. I caught on a nail."

❦ A different order of being ❧

God is a different order of being. He is Being Itself.

On the level where we are today (God operates on a vast variety of levels, and reveals Himself differently on all) God operates as law more than He does as a person.

He has to reveal Himself to us in a form we can grasp.

Infinity is not easy for a finite mind to lay hold of. Someone has said that it is like trying to take the temperature of the sun with an ordinary thermometer.

This is not too hard at a distance of 93,000,000 miles where we see the sun merely as a brilliant orb in the sky and experience its life-giving warmth and light.

But when we come too close to the sun, the beneficent life-giving warmth and light become a raging, life-destroying furnace of atomic power.

The sun, too, is a different order of being, and we have to communicate with it—and live with it—for the most part—on its terms.

God in His entirety is beyond our power to grasp or touch. But beholding him as a warm, bright, distant orb in the heavens, we reduce Him to something within our power to live by.

Men have continually reduced God to a personal form.

A Hindu heretic, Gautama Siddartha, trying to keep men from doing this, even taught that the Eternal itself is a doubtful concept. "Of changeless, fixed being I see no sign," he said. But men laid hold of Gautama Siddartha, proclaimed him the Buddha, made golden idols of him, and placed him in ten thousand shining temples.

They even fashioned thousands of other Buddhas besides him—some of them not too human in form, but recognizable.

Most Christians find it easier to think of Jesus and to turn to Him than to God; many find it easier to turn to Mary or to a saint.

We want to bring God down closer to our level and make Him more like ourselves.

Perhaps, what He would like is for us to make an effort to rise to His level and become more like Him.

৺ৡ Principles act ৢ৶

If we go to God as if He were a person, we should not be surprised if He acts like one. We think of Him, of course, as a divine Person. Perhaps it is better to say as a Personage, at least the equal of a King or the President. So we should not be surprised if He is not easily accessible. We would not have much luck getting into Buckingham Palace or the White House—and Heaven, as we generally think of it, is even farther away and harder to get to than they are. From all we have been told, its portals are carefully guarded and few of us will get through them.

If we think of God as a Person, then we can expect that sometimes He will respond to us and sometimes he will not.

But when we think of God as Principle, immediately we see that we have to approach Him in a different way and He will respond to us in a different way.

Principles do not go into action because we beg them to. They act because they are already and always in action.

Principles act because they are there.

And they act for us because we conform to them.

Every law in the universe—if it is a law—is constantly in operation.

It operates in our life. It operates when we ask it to. It operates when we do not ask it to.

It works for us when we align ourselves with it. But it does not stop working when we do not align ourselves with it.

It does not alter itself to conform to our will; it does not do our bidding because we ask it to; but when we do what is necessary to bring its action into our life, it acts unfailingly to produce results.

Electricity, for instance, is a principle. Actually, it is an unknown principle. It is merely a form of energy that exists in the universe. No one knows what it is. The most learned physicists do not know what it is. They merely have found that an unknown principle which exists in nature reveals its presence and acts to make light or heat or power when they perform certain acts and set certain kinds of machines in operation.

At the present time, the machines we use to get this principle we call electricity to work for us are primitive, almost as much as the witch doctors' amulets and dances were.

But they work, if not too efficiently, and we will find better ways as we work with them.

They work, of course, for everyone who works with them.

ᴕᴈ *The rain falls* ᴂᴖ

The rain falls on the just and the unjust.

God, as law, as principle, does His perfect work for all who avail themselves of the power of the law. He operates as law operates, not as a person operates.

We conform to the law, we place ourselves in alignment with the principle at work, and the whole power of the universe is set in action to carry us to fulfillment.

You can see that prayer is not at all the same thing when you are conforming to a Principle as when you are calling out to a Person.

If there is a Law that works for good in the world and if it works through us when we put ourselves in harmony with it by keeping our thoughts, words, and actions aligned with good—and both our reason and the evidence of men's lives indicate that there is such a law—then we have to align our thoughts, words, and actions to conform with the good and keep them aligned with the good. We have to keep them aligned whatever happens, and continue to keep them aligned.

And by a law that works for good, I mean a law that works to increase life, love, energy, intelligence, joy, order, beauty.

Most of the time we think thoughts that are not aligned with the good; we work against ourselves; we work against the will of life; we set destructive powers at work in our life rather than constructive ones.

Certainly, it should not surprise us, then, when we reap destructive results.

We feel hatred and hostility—why would we not expect hatred and hostility to spill into our lives?

We feel fear and frustration—why would we not expect to be frustrated and troubled of mind?

We cling to outdated ways of believing and living—why would we not expect life to walk away from us?

The fact that we pray and nothing seems to happen is not nearly so important or meaningful as the fact that we pray and something does happen.

If one person has ever gotten healing because he prayed, it proves that a principle is there that heals when we learn how to let it work through us and for us.

If one person has ever had a need supplied because he prayed, it proves that a principle is there that supplies our needs when we know how to let it work.

If one person has ever met a problem because he prayed, it

proves that a principle exists that will enable us to meet our problems.

We knew electricity was there for years before we learned how to put it to constructive uses. We saw lightning flash—interestingly, we thought of it as the activity of a person-god—of Zeus, or Thor, or Indra.

Interestingly, too, we saw the electric principle working in destructive ways—setting fires and hurting people—long before we saw how to use it in constructive ways.

✦§ Not because we coax it §✦

Divine law does not work for us because we coax it.

It does not work because we threaten it.

It does not work because we perform certain rites or because we pay others to perform these rites.

It works because we conform to it.

How does any law work for us?

Let us look at one.

Newton's Third Law of Motion states that every force exerts an equal and opposite force.

First, we have to understand what the principle is.

Then, we seek for methods of using it—techniques and machines that put it to work for us.

Also, we look at the world around us in the light of this principle.

Knowledge of the principle enables us to see more clearly into the modus operandi of things, into the way things work, and into the way they are put together.

It gives us a clearer notion of what our world is really like.

It enables us to build machines—even at last rockets that will lift us off the earth—that greatly increase our power over life and the world around us.

It should be considered that if God is to be thought of as law, He is not *a* law. He is intelligence and love and power expressing themselves in a way that we call law.

He is law wherever you find it. By law, I do not mean man-made statutes, but the principles on which the universe is run, the rules by which it is regulated.

To say that God is law means that we see deity operating as law. We conceive that which runs the universe to be law.

This is certainly the scientific way of looking at the world, is it not?

VII

IN THE WORLD OR OUT OF IT

❧ A science and an art ❧

I said to the Master,
"Is prayer a science or an art?"
The Master said,
"Is healing a science or an art? Let us be glad that it is both."
At the present time, prayer is not so much a matter of systematic study of law as of lucky hits.
Sometimes we touch through to reality; much of the time we do not.
Prayer is more an art than it is a science.
At the present time, we have to be happy with the lucky hits as well as with the systematic discoveries—but at the present time so does science.
We have to work at the art of prayer along with the science of prayer.
Let us perfect the art and unfold the science.
Let us pray. Let us practice prayer.
At the level where we are.
Because this is the only place we can start.
We cannot start from where we are not.
Pray. Pray now. Pray as best you know how.
But as you pray, pray knowing that prayer has laws to be discovered and ways to be perfected.
Its techniques have not all been found.
Man is seeking to lay hold of the power he knows lies all around him and within him.
He is seeking to lay hold of the intelligence he senses is operating through things and himself.
He is seeking to lay hold of more and more life, because he senses that life is coming into ever fuller expression.

And dimly most of the time, but vividly sometimes, he senses that through and over and in all things—and most of all in himself—there is a Love at work.

This, too, he yearns with a deep and burning longing to touch and develop in himself.

There can be no doubt that prayer and meditation are a means to uncovering and laying hold of this power, life, intelligence, and love.

Considering prayer and meditation in their largest sense, I wonder if man has ever increased his knowledge and dominion over himself and his world in any other way except through prayer and meditation.

Some man went about his daily tasks listening and inviting and considering, and suddenly he exclaimed, "I see. I know."

After that, man had new access to power or intelligence or life or love.

Prayer is a ladder.

Every prayer we make lifts us to a higher rung—a higher power, a higher truth, a higher vision, a higher faith.

Every prayer we make is a step we take closer to God.

✢§ My father and my mother §✢

Prayer is a ladder.

We lean it up against the world and climb up on it.

We climb up on it and try to get a new view of things.

We climb up on it and try to fix the gutters of our thought or repair the roof of our life.

In our time we have come up with new ideas as to how to build the ladder.

Many Western thinkers, disenchanted with the primitive notions they were taught in their Sunday School, have turned to the East for instruction. They feel that the East knows more about prayer than Western orthodoxy does.

Certainly the East has a great deal to tell us about how to build the ladder of prayer—or would it be more exact to call it the way of meditation?

It is no accident that every great religion that has won wide assent from human beings has sprung out of Asia.

The West has achieved great triumphs of thought. In the West, we have given our best minds to business and science—and the achievements of business and science gleam brilliantly around us. We have erected a tremendous technological civilization. We have built fantastic machines capable of blowing up a world and rocketing us into space. We have fed and clothed and sheltered ourselves almost beyond our dreams. Our cities glitter over earth like jewels.

But for thousands of years, in India especially, after a man has met his obligations to the human community—raised his sons and provided for his family—he has been allowed to withdraw from the world around him, to become a forest-wanderer, a beggar, a holy man, and to seek inside himself the essential meaning of himself and his relation to the world.

Through the centuries, many of the most intelligent men of India have followed this custom. Only a few years back, my local newspaper carried a story about a member of Nehru's cabinet who was resigning to go into the jungle, there to live out his life in solitary thought.

The Hindus have given their best minds to introspective analysis—the study of the self and its relation to the world around it. Naturally, this Hindu custom has produced results.

Western psychologists have only yesterday landed on the shore of man's unconscious. Most of them still have no awareness of the extent of their discovery; like Columbus, they imagine they have landed on some small spice island, when in truth they have discovered a continent.

The Hindus got here long ago. Two thousand years before Freud, their thinkers made their introspective journey, went deep into the unknown land they found, mapped many of its mysteries, and gave its mountains and its rivers names.

What is man's mind, soul, psyche, self, buddhi, atman—call it what you will?

As Western psychologists probe into man, I have a hunch they will find that what the Hindus have learned is correct. We will only corroborate their findings and put them in scientific terms rather than in religious and mystical ones.

The East has achieved brilliant insights. In recent years, more and more Westerners have been studying them.

But illuminating as some of the findings of the East have

been, and willing as I am to praise them, the basic insight of the East I reject.

For the basic insight of the East rejects life.

Buddhism has taken many forms. Hinduism has taken many forms. But wherever you find the Eastern approach to life—whether it be Buddhist, or Hindu, or Taoist—when you get to the heart of it, you find that it rejects life.

The purpose of life, in the Eastern view—however complicatedly and obscurely the literature may disguise it, when you get to the root of it, there it is—the purpose of life, in the Eastern view, is to learn how to escape from living. The Easterner's ideal man is the holy man—the *sannyasin*, the *yogin*, the *tirthankara*—sitting immovable in the silence, having withdrawn not only from the world, but from his self.

I do not accept this as an ideal.

We do not find ourselves alive in order to reject life.

We have not been given the gift of the word—the unbelievable gift of communication—in order to be silent—golden though silence may sometimes be.

We do not possess these hands, "these pickers and stealers," in order to sit on them—another part of our anatomy suffices for sitting.

I do not believe any of this.

Every ounce of my logicality and every inch of my aliveness joins in disbelief.

All my observation of living things says No to it.

All my feeling about life says No to it.

All my living of life says No to it.

When the Hindus tell me life is for withdrawing, I say No. I say No, too, when I find such notions in the religious and metaphysical thinking of the West.

Many religious thinkers in the West have taught that this life is merely a brief prelude to the real life. This life is merely a painful trial through which we have to pass, a trial we only pass through successfully by denying that it has worth and importance, and living as if it had none.

I do not believe this.

I was not born into this world in order to escape from it or to live as if it were not there.

All you saints and sannyasins, Christian or Hindu—you world deniers—though you rail at me from every temple and prove to me in ten thousand scriptures that my purpose is to deny the world, I shall never believe you.

If God is my father, this world is my mother. Its seas surge in my veins; its winds blow through my longings.

I would not deny my father; I believe that He is God. But neither shall I deny my mother; she—this lovely world—is also God. If Brahma is the reality of appearances, Maya is the appearance of reality.

I am the child of the Infinite, but I am also the child of the Finite—and I find meaning in both my aspects.

Indeed, I only find meaning in their union. For it is only their union that brings me into being.

A digression on the divine feminine

An interesting thought I merely drop into your mind—a pebble in a pool, I hope, to ripple out, to make you want to follow the ripple.

The Hindus call this space-time world of appearances, of shapes and thoughts, maya.

What a lovely name!

To the Hindus *maya* is the feminine aspect of reality.

We have named our loveliest month after this divine feminine —May, the mothering month.

We probably got our word from the Greek word, Maia—the beautiful mother of a god—but this is a sister word to the Sanskrit, as is that first word of every tongue, Ma.

If you happen to believe that we got May from *Maius,* which is the Latin for *great,* it makes no difference; we get our words *magic* and *might* and *mother* from the same motherly root.

Maya is the feminine aspect of reality, the creative reproductive energy of the world.

Is not this energy the mightiest and most magical force there is?

You may think of maya as this world or as the metaphysical matrix out of which the world comes.

Maya is the appearance; maya is the magic power that creates the appearance.

Out of this world-womb all forms flow—all the ten thousand things of this world that, even as we look, disappear as at a wave of a magician's wand and are changed into ten thousand other things.

Ma, Maia, maya—this is the Maiden Mother of a thousand names and faces, spinner of seasons and cycles, womb of all finite things and thoughts, shaper and shapes, dreamer and dreams, this ever-turning, overturning world of change!

Whatever name we give her, she is ever the Immortal Consort of the Eternal One. Mother Earth and Queen of Heaven—Parvati, Kwanyin, Frigga, Anahita, Ishtar, Isis, Gaea, Kybele—she has as many forms as the changing world she represents, and is worshiped by one name or another in every great religion the world has seen.

The Hindus were metaphysicians even more than they were myth-makers—and they had plenty of names, lovely and frightful, for the Mother Goddess. They saw her as beautiful witch or stately goddess or hideous hag, as she may variously appear to you.

For it makes a great deal of difference whether she comes to you as Isis or Kybele, as Kwanyin or Kali.

Persephone is the red-lipped, warm, and comely spring, but she is also the pale-cheeked guardian of the gate of death.

It is an ancient way of saying that this world of shifting shapes and thoughts, is a world of change. Spring moves on till it is winter. Day turns into night. She who gives birth also gives death. To be born is to die. But to die is to be born!

◦⸱ A further digression on truths ⸱◦

I hope that you have not been brainwashed by the Western illusion that truth can only be stated in a scientific formula or as historical fact, and so dismiss stories like the tale of a Virgin Mother as foolish fable.

What a limited view of things to believe that truth is always facts or that facts are always true!

St. George and his dragon are just as real as an atom.

Genesis is just as true as Darwin's *Origin of the Species*.

And the Easter story has much more truth in it than, for instance, Josephus' "History of the Jews," which makes doubtful mention of it.

Long before he knew anything about scientific formulas or historical facts, man was finding truths and trying to express them.

He has painted them and sung them and recited them and acted them out in rites.

He was doing this before he had words to express truth in.

Without words he was expressing truth very well.

Words are at most secondhand conveyors of truth.

They serve best in intellectual matters, which are only a small part of our concern.

Try to tell me what spring is like, for instance.

Spring is certainly a truth—I don't believe anyone would deny this.

To tell me what spring is like, you are going to have to write a lot of books about astronomy and the earth's orbit around the sun and the equinox and meteorology and the movement of air masses and biology and migratory birds and recurring vegetation—and I wonder after all your mountain of books if I will have even the foggiest notion what spring is. I don't care how many scientific formulas you give me for chlorophyll and photosynthesis and mitosis—and how many historical facts as to the exact day and hour when the swallows come back to Capistrano.

You would do better to have a poet read me a poem or a painter paint me a picture.

Go out and fetch me a handful of daffodils or violets, or a broken branch of pussy willow or peach blossoms—and I have the truth of spring itself.

Or take me out to frolic with you across the fields and woods of a May morning.

That will be truth enough for me.

Or let us consider a drink of cold water.

There is no question, is there, that water quenches thirst?

This is a truth—and man has known it long before he was man. My cat knows it. Any flying bug knows it. Even the willow tree that clogs my sewer knows it.

But I defy you to convey this truth to me by talking to me about the physical and chemical properties of water and the human body. You can talk about specific gravity and H_2O and cell structure and osmosis till your throat is dry—and I will know little more about the power of water to quench thirst than I did when you began.

Pour me a glass of cold water from your pitcher and let me drink—and you need say nothing at all.

Or take love—the love of a young man and a young woman.

I am sure that physiology textbooks and psychology textbooks can give me useful information. But love—physical love—is more than anything a tumult in the blood, a fire in the flesh, a drunkenness of spirit and conscription of the mind that overpower a whole world of regimented Nay-saying to plant love's lusty Yea in the central citadel of life.

Prayer is related to the class of truths that love and spring and a drink of cold water belong to.

The very word *miracle* has a kind of unscientific, unhistorical air about it.

So does God, when you come to think of it. But the fact that I cannot express Him in a mathematical equation or write His definitive biography does not make Him less real. It makes Him more real. It makes Him more God.

I can know him not by reading a book about Him, but by reaching out to Him.

Then he becomes as real as spring, as love, as a drink of cold water.

He is a drink of cold water when I am spiritually thirsty—a drink of living water.

I can reach out to Him in prayer.

And so can you.

❧ The world I live in ❧

But let us return to the road we were on before I took us for a walk in the Elysian fields of myth and truth. As I tell you elsewhere in this book, in my kind of thinking you never know till you have done it whether you are going to cross the brook or walk along its banks, stay on the road or strike off through the woods.

As I was saying before I struck off through the woods, I do not find myself in this world, so much a part of it and it so much a part of me, in order to act as if it were not there; to deny its reality; and to live as little in it as I can.

I am not intended to do as little as I can. I am intended to do as much as I can.

The world is here to be accepted.

To be lived in.

To be worked with.

The world is not expected to be the same when I go out of it as it was when I came into it—and, of course, it never is.

The world is to grow.

What I do is a stage in its growth.

For the world shapes me, but also in my turn I shape it.

Beautiful as the world is, I come so that it may become yet more beautiful.

Varied as its thoughts and things are, I come to think yet more thoughts, fashion yet more things.

Manifold as are its works, I come to work yet more works.

Are there cities?

I shall build higher towers, broader avenues, houses more fitting to be the dwellings of men.

Are there gardens?

I shall put a wall around waste places. I shall water and till until the desert becomes a green-gold sea of wheat and corn, and the wilderness blossoms and bears fruit.

I shall drain the marshes.

I shall master the mountains.

Is there ugliness?

I shall turn it into beauty.

Is there sickness?

I shall change it into health.

Is there death?

I shall bring it back to life.

I shall give peace for pain and joy for loneliness. I shall turn darkness into light.

I shall multiply the few loaves and fishes into abundance for the nations.

I shall dare the dark and walk among the stars. I shall venture into vastness.

Are there unknown worlds? I shall make them known.

Are there mysteries? I shall turn them into truths.

The world is mine to pray and work and live in.

I have hands for handling it.

I have feet for traveling through it.

I have a mind equipped for looking at it, understanding it, turning its stuff into thoughts and turning thoughts into the stuff of a new and better world.

All of me all together, I am made to live in it and to make it more alive!

I was formed for lifting, and bearing, and breaking things apart, and putting things together.

I think.

I speak.

Even more, I do.

Though it may be that I am because I think, it is only because I do that I am anything worth being. "I think, therefore I am," said Descartes. But I say, "I am, therefore I do."

If we try to make of our prayer a mountaintop for meditation, one day prayer will drive us down our mountain and into the river that runs through the teeming valley at its foot, to rescue those who are struggling there for life.

The highest purpose of prayer and the highest purpose of life is not sitting in silence, not spiritual meditation, not knowing the truth; it is living the life.

The most fortunate of men have always been the doers.

Mahomet, Moses, Confucius, Jesus—they are not great because they knew God but because they changed life! Our life, yours and mine.

The world has not been the same since they lived in it.

That is why we honor and revere them—even worship them as gods.

Godlike, they changed the world.

They were men of prayer—or meditation, whichever you like to call it.

But prayer was not for any of them an end in itself.

They prayed so that they could live and help others to live a more alive life.

Even the Buddha, who taught world-denial and withdrawal, did not himself withdraw. Having found his truth, he did not sit in silent contemplation of it.

In the story—remember?—he sat down under a fig tree and there reached enlightenment. There he became free of the world. The world had no power over him any longer; he could withdraw from it if he wished.

He cried out to life and himself:

"Broken thy house is, and the ridge-pole split!

"Delusion fashioned it!

"Safe pass I thence—deliverance to obtain."

But he did not pass.

As he sat there, the first question he asked himself was whether he should withdraw or not. Should he abstract himself from this world of suffering, as he now had power to do—or should he plunge back into the world, so full of pain and imperfections, to help his fellow men?

The Buddha scarcely hesitated.

He came back from the fig tree into the world of men and lived in it earnestly. Every day he went into the streets with his begging bowl. There he rubbed shoulders and thoughts with the humblest people and the proudest people. He taught. He admonished. He rebuked. He inspired. He even organized the order of monks that ever since has spread his teaching.

When he was eighty years old—forty-five strenuous years after having found the truth that was to have freed him from this world—he was still living a full, active life; and he was on a long hard journey by foot, teaching and visiting friends who needed his help, when at last death overtook him.

Enlightenment is good.

But it is not a world set free.

A blueprint is good.

But it is not a house.

A grain of wheat is good.

But it is not a loaf of bread.

A silent thought is good.

But it is not the touch of a loving hand.

There is a prayer that is sitting in the silence.

But there is also a prayer that is living and doing and striving and working and walking on.

And the prayer that is silence is not complete until it becomes the prayer that is a life fully lived.

VIII

WORK IS A PRAYER

◄§ *The Master sat silent* §►

I said to the Master, "Shall I do outer things as well as sit in silent meditation and pray?"

The Master sat silent.

After a time I said again, "Please, Master. Shall I do outer things as well as pray?"

The Master continued to sit silent.

I reached out and caught His sleeve, and I said once more, louder than before, "Master, Master, answer me."

Then he said, "Is not your own insistence that I speak to you your answer? Here I sit in silent meditation. But you would have me do more. You would have me speak to you."

Life is not for praying; prayer is for living. Prayer is part of life —and should be part of life—but life is more than prayer.

Life halloos in your ear and tugs at your sleeve and beckons you to be up and at your tasks.

Go sit in silent meditation on an anthill—and then ask your question.

If a man comes to us for help, let us help him in every way we can.

If a man comes hungry, and I have food, what kind of prayer will I make, feasting at my laden table, staring at his gaunt face? To share my food with him, and also to share my heart with him— what prayer is more powerful than this?

How can I feed the man if I do not love him, and how can I love the man if I do not feed him?

For the bread I give him without love will be a beggar's bread and will leave him starving of spirit. And the love I give him without bread will be a miser's love and will leave me starving of spirit.

If we can bind up wounds, dare we leave another bleeding?

If we can speak words of courage, dare we leave another without hope?

If we have a hand to reach and a heart to give, dare we leave another in the pit?

And if we are ourself the one in the pit, then let us reach out our hand to help ourself.

Life has not given us these hands merely to fold in prayer. Life has not given us this heart that it should harden itself against pity.

Life has given us imagination and courage and love and strength to devise and dare and carry out.

Whatever we have to do, let us do everything we can. If we cannot do anything, let us stand and wait!

Standing and waiting can be a kind of doing, too.

We can pray when we are standing and waiting. We can pray when we are digging and building and running and lifting, too.

Always we should do all we can.

To go beyond our own resources, we have first to come to the end of them.

Sir Ian Fleming discovered penicillin when a mold got into his test tube. But Sir Ian Fleming had been seeking healing agents all his life!

Charles Goodyear discovered how to vulcanize rubber when he happened to be cooking a stew pot full of the stuff and some ran over on the kitchen stove. But Charles Goodyear had spent twenty years and all his fortune trying to find how to vulcanize rubber!

William Roentgen discovered X-rays when a plate left in a drawer was mysteriously fogged one night. But William Roentgen had given his whole life and all his energies to learning more about the nature of things!

When David went out against Goliath, I am sure He prayed—David was a praying man—but also he used what he had to use. This was not much, a sling and a stone, but he used it—and it was enough.

To pray is to ask and affirm.

To pray is also to sow and till.

For to ask and affirm is to sow and till in spirit.

And to sow and till is to ask and affirm of the earth.

When the inward and the outward man are one, then we pray with our whole being. When our whole being moves in one direction, then all the forces of life are drawn together and rush forward to bring the prayer we make to fruition.

❧ *With a hammer and a hoe* ❧

Three men were fishing in a small boat on a lake when a storm arose. The winds rocked the boat, the waves washed over the sides, and the boat began to take on water.

"We had better pray," cried the first man.

"We had better bail," cried the second man.

"Let us pray," said the third man, "but let us bail while we pray."

There is a prayer that is action.

Too often we think we cannot pray unless we are sitting still, eyes closed, body relaxed, thought suspended.

We are right to think that prayer is stillness, but stillness is not all that prayer is. Prayer is action, too.

And is not stillness part of action?

The Hindus say that there are four roads to fulfillment. One of them is the road of action or work.

To work with no attachment to your work is to reach God.

This is the way a bird sings. It lights on a bough, bursts into song, and having finished, flies on, not looking back for payment or applause. Perhaps, after a while, it will light on another bough —and sing again—but it will not be the same song.

This is the way a flower blooms. It opens its petals, pours out its fragrance, gives itself to any passing bee or butterfly or breeze, and then, letting its petals one by one flutter to the ground, is gone. Perhaps, after a while, it may bloom again— but it will not be the same bloom.

This is the way a man works, too, when he works at his highest pitch. He gives himself to what he is doing; he lets himself be used; he becomes a free channel through which ideas and energy flow.

And you do this, not for the results you are going to gain from your work, but for the joy-in-work itself. You do it because you are a working part of the great works we call the world.

This is the way a man builds a dam or a bridge—or irrigates a desert or reclaims a marsh.

This is the way a man plants a tree—for the joy of being part of life.

It matters little that he may never sit under its shade or see its flowers in spring or pluck fruit from its branches.

The best work that men do is done because it is the nature of men to work. There is the chasm to be spanned. There is the desert to be watered.

"Why do you want to climb the mountain?" we ask the mountain climber.

"Because it is there," he answers.

And climbing the mountain is as much a way of prayer as sitting still and speaking words.

Every refusal to turn back in the face of difficulty is a denial of those forces that forever gnaw at the edge of enterprise to thwart and wear away the questing spirit of man.

Every dogged step is an affirmation of faith in life and of the value of life.

There are people who are not articulate; they are doers more than speakers; people of deeds rather than words.

But God accepts the prayers of their wordless hands just as joyously as He accepts the speech of the word-sayers.

God finds all gifts good, and there are many ways to Him.

Apples are good, but grain and grass are not less good.

Redbirds are good, but earthworms are not less good.

They are different. That is all.

A friend of mine lost his son. He did not say much to anyone, but the next day he began to repaper the rooms of his house. He worked until every wall in his house had new paper on it.

I cannot believe that his work was not as acceptable an offering to his God as if he had gone wailing on his knees, lighting candles, beating his heart, and intoning Kyrie eleisons.

A minister asked the people of a country community to pray for the poor in the community. Several members of the church gathered and were praying when a boy appeared.

"My father could not come to pray," he said, "so he sent what he could." Outside the church was a wagon loaded with food.

Which is the greater prayer for another—words of blessing you may speak for him or acts of love you may do for him?

"Without God, we cannot," someone has said. "Without us, God will not."

God will not do the work for us, but He will work through us.

God will not make the world a better place for us to live in, but He will give us the power to make it a better place.

A man bought a run-down farm. The land was weed-infested, rock-ridden, eroded, depleted. The buildings were falling down. After long labor he turned it into a model farm. He repaired the buildings. He dug the weeds and rocks out of his fields. He dammed up the wasting waters. He rebuilt the wasted soil.

One day his minister visited him.

"What a beautiful farm God and you have here," said the minister.

"So it is," said the man.

"I know how much this place has meant to you," said the minister. "You must have prayed about it a great deal."

"I have that," said the man. "And I did most of my praying with a hammer and a hoe."

Only God can make a tree, but if you want an apple orchard, someone has to work very hard.

❧ An electrochemical machine ❧

You are, in a physical sense, a kind of electrochemical machine.

You eat. You drink. You breathe.

Food and water and air are carried through various ducts of your body to your cells. There they are mixed and burned.

Every cell in your body is a minute furnace.

In every one of them a fire is burning.

From those fires energy radiates.

What you do with this energy determines your life.

You can put the energy to profitable uses.

You can put the energy to unprofitable uses.

You have energy.

You produce more energy constantly.

The use you put your energy to—this determines whether your life is happy or unhappy.

One of the great purposes of prayer is to help us to put our energies to constructive uses.

We all need energy.

We all have things to do.

We have joyous occasions that we want to celebrate.

We have hard trials we have to meet.

We have problems we have to solve.

We have problems we do not know how to solve.

Gratification, success, achievement, celebration—these are usually—not always!—easy to handle.

But in most lives, along with these, we are also called to meet frustration, failure, disappointment, sorrow.

At times, we get what we do not want, and what we want we do not get.

On these occasions, we may use our energy in various ways.

We may get drunk or turn to drugs.

We may get sick, physically or mentally.

We may shoot somebody or ourself.

We may curse or write a letter to an editor.

We may beat our children or our wife, or fight with a friend or our boss, or even foment a riot.

On the other hand, we may paper our house or chop a tree into firewood or play a round of golf.

We may talk things over with an understanding friend.

We may write a book.

We may go for a hike or take a trip.

We may pray.

Sometimes I wonder what people do who have not learned to pray. How do they meet disappointment and loss?

It is not that I always get what I pray for.

Certainly I have not.

But prayer itself is its own answer to prayer.

Prayer itself is a way of meeting life, of meeting trials, and coming up through them and coming up over them.

It is blessed to have your prayers answered, but it is blessed just to pray.

You can live without praying.

But you cannot live as well.

You can live with one eye or one hand. You can live without taking thought.

You can live without giving attention to your body or your mind or your spirit.

But you cannot live well.

And I think that life without eyes or hands, hard as it might be, would not be so empty as a life lacking spiritual dimension. You are a spiritual being living in a spiritual world, whether you want to be or not; your soul may suffer from hidden hungers, as much as your body can. When you do not drink, you thirst, though you may not know what you thirst for.

You thirst for prayer.

❦ When you do not know what to do ❧

What do you do when you come on times when you do not know what to do?

What action do you take when you see no useful course of action?

When you find yourself having to meet some condition that you yourself have no power to meet, what do you meet it with?

How fortunate you are if you have learned to pray.

For if you have learned to pray, you have learned to still your apprehension, relax your body and thought, turn your attention away from your problems and toward God. You have learned to concentrate your thinking toward Him, looking, waiting, expecting, willing—and confident that He is your help in time of trouble!

You have learned to think what is good; you have learned to expect what is good; you have learned to call forth what is good.

In a cartoon drawing, two prisoners lie manacled and in leg irons on a dungeon floor. They are in rags. Their matted beard and hair have grown down to their waists. They are hollow-eyed, skeleton-thin. One of them has turned his head to the other and is saying, "Now, here's my plan!"

There is a sense in which all of us are in a prison. The prison is ourself, the dungeon is our loneliness.

I do not know the way out. But I know there is a way.

What are you doing to extricate yourself from your own pettiness?

And when you have become more, what are you going to make of your greatness?

The Count of Monte Cristo, in Dumas' tale, lived for revenge. But this twisted hope was enough to get him out of his unbelievable dungeon and to make him one of the richest men on earth.

In World War II those in prison camps who survived in good health were those who survived in good spirits.

They had not given up.

They had looked forward to release.

They had planned what their life would be when they were free again.

They had kept faith.

In 1958 in Nova Scotia, a mine explosion imprisoned seven men for nine days in total darkness, hundreds of feet below the surface, sealed off completely from any communication with the surface, in tiny pockets of blackness so small they could not stand. They had no food. They had no water. They did not know what condition the explosion had left in the mine. They did not know whether attempts at rescue were being made or not. They did not know whether it was even possible for attempts at rescue to be made.

In these conditions they survived nine days.

They sang hymns.

They prayed.

When one of them began to lose faith and show fear, the others gathered around him and took turns telling all the stories they knew of men who had been rescued from mine disasters.

A man was imprisoned in a French prison. He was confined to one small cell.

In the cell was one window.

By standing on a stool he could look out.

The scene the man saw from the window he painted. He

painted it over and over. He painted it on any material he could paint on. He painted it in all seasons and in all moods. And he left the painting for those who came after him to catch faith from.

In 1949 an English woman, Dr. Edith Bone, was imprisoned in Hungary and spent seven years in solitary confinement. At first to keep busy, she recited poetry to herself. She spoke six languages, so she translated the poems from one language to another.

Confined to a cell 5'×10', she walked home to England in her mind. She knew how far it was to the Hungarian border, to Vienna, to Calais. Some days she would walk as much as twenty miles. Back and forth in her 5'×10' cell her legs carried her—but in her mind she journeyed freely and joyously across Europe.

Each day she knew exactly what scenes she was walking through; for she paced the distance and kept count on an abacus of how far she walked and where she was. This abacus she made out of pellets of the inedible black bread, which was her daily meal, and straws from a broom, with which she had to keep her cell clean.

On her abacus, she made inventories of the words she knew in all her six languages, counting up to 27,369 words in English. She did many other things. She refused to let her interests waste away; she kept herself linked with life.

Dr. Bone was sixty-one when she was imprisoned. Seven years later, when the Hungarian revolution of 1956 freed her and she was able to escape to England, she was still healthy, vigorous, alert, alive.

What have these stories to do with prayer? you may ask.

I suppose, if you think of prayer as merely a formal request made on an external God, they have nothing to do with prayer.

But to me these stories express the very essence of prayer.

Prayer is keeping faith.

Prayer is meeting things hard to meet with a confident, hopeful attitude.

We may use fixed forms and special words to help us keep this attitude.

We may just keep the attitude.

Both the words and the attitude are prayer.

You pray when you turn your thought to life.

You pray when you love.

You pray when you express beauty and truth.

You pray when you hold to hope or stand firm in faith.

You pray when you have patience and fortitude.

You pray when you expect good.

You pray when you stay stronger than circumstance and reach beyond limitations with your mind and with your spirit.

You pray when you refuse to give up, when you keep on, when you go forward. When circumstance stops you from doing this physically, you pray when you keep on going forward in mind and spirit.

Prayer is itself a profitable use of your energy.

All of us are most inclined to pray when we do not know what else to do.

We are much like the frightened lady in the storm-battered ship. When she asked the Captain what she could do and he told her, "Madam, you can pray," she cried out:

"Good heavens, Captain, is it as bad as that?"

As long as we can see something to do, we do it. It is only when we are at a loss as to what to do, only when we do not know where to turn, that we are likely to turn to prayer.

But this is one reason the habit of prayer is so valuable.

Energy does not stop flowing because we are not directing and using it. It flows just the same. In fact, in times of crisis, the flow of energy increases.

Crisis is a storm. In a storm, the wind blows and the rain falls harder than at any other time. The waters in the stream rise.

But when we do not know what to do, when we see no course of action to take, it is as if we had thrown a dam across the stream of life.

Behind it the debris-packed, rushing water backs up, higher and higher and higher.

If we do not take control, if we do not direct this swirling energy somewhere, it may overflow our banks and flood our world with muddy ruin or it may smash through the dam and wreck everything in its path.

But prayer is like a sluice gate. When the storm comes and the waters begin to rise, we open the gate of prayer and the water flows gently, steadily where we want it to go—into paths of constructive thinking—thinking about God, about life, about love, about power; into looking and listening for inspiration and instruction; into finding faith and joy; into positive thinking instead of negative resisting.

As the water runs down this course our prayers have dug for it, we find ways to use it profitably—to irrigate our emptiness, to turn our mills of creative thinking, to quench our thirst for spiritual knowledge and power, and to carry us into communication with others around us.

⇜ Prayer is a balance ⇝

Power is transmitted by the wheel at its swiftly moving circumference, but the power comes from the hub that does not move at all.

The more power there is at the edge of the wheel, the more necessary it is for the hub to be still. The slightest motion—the least jiggle—at the hub of a great flywheel would quickly shake the wheel to pieces.

High achievement comes only out of intense effort. But intense effort comes only out of a still, poised, relaxed attitude.

To reach the shore a swimmer has to relax his body and let the water hold him up. Then he moves rhythmically—feet, arms, body, breath, harmoniously together. The more he lets the water hold him up, the more he is able to let all parts of his body move together effortlessly without thought. In other words, the more still he becomes, the more swiftly he gets through the water.

The great runner is not the one with whom every step is a studied effort, but the one whose every step is effortlessly free.

The inspired man hits the mark without taking aim.

Jesus turned within and prayed. Then He turned without and taught and healed. But his turning out was no less part of communing with God than was His turning in.

I breathe in; then I breathe out again. Breathing out is as much a part of breathing as breathing in is.

Likewise, I need to feel that my work is no less a prayer than my silent sitting.

I am as close to God when I sow seed in my garden or till the earth or write a book or fix a machine or cook a meal or clean a house as I am when I get still to pray.

If I am not close to Him then, will I be close when I get still?

And what will getting still avail me? I can only spend a small part of my life in stillness. Am I supposed to spend the main part of my life separated from God?

If I do not learn to touch God, to live close to God, when I am moving and doing, playing and working and loving and living, I shall touch Him very little—and He will touch me very little.

I turn to God consciously and in the silence so that I can carry about with me the awareness of His presence and power in all my daily acts.

I need to be close to God all the time. I need to see that prayer is sitting in silent meditation and prayer is doing everything that has to be done by me. Prayer, at its highest, is a balance.

Is it truer to say that the earth forms the tree out of itself so that it may find expression, or that the tree forms the earth into itself so that it may be expressed?

Prayer is using all the forces of life, and prayer is letting all the forces of life use me.

Prayer is willing, and prayer is being willing. Prayer is working, and prayer is letting. Prayer is asserting, and prayer is assenting.

Prayer does everything, yet does not seem to move. Prayer does nothing, yet gets everything done. Prayer is the activity that is stillness, and the stillness that is activity. When prayer is at its best, stillness flows into activity and activity flows into stillness.

Prayer is the bird with wings outspread effortlessly soaring in the summer afternoon. But first the bird must learn to fly.

Perhaps prayer is most of all like a journey that we take by airplane.

We climb into the plane and strap ourselves into the seat. It may take a little time to get the plane onto the runway. We may have to start and wait; we may have to let our motors roar and idle and roar again. Then all at once we are taking off; we have to look to know we are in the air. We have no sense of rising, but in minutes we have risen above the clouds.

Then there we float, though we know we are not floating. We

have no sense of speed, yet we know that we are moving at incredible speed. There is no feeling of activity, yet we know that much is happening.

We sit motionless in our seat. Outside the window, if we look, cloud shapes form and melt and form again. Nothing moves. We do not move. The plane does not move. The world does not move. Yet space is obliterated. Time is pressed in upon itself until it almost disappears.

The plane vibrates as if in a vacuum, and we float through a nothingness of neverwhen, where everything hangs suspended, everything waits. We do nothing. We go nowhere. Yet doing nothing, going nowhere, all at once we are coming down upon our destination.

Though I know no rocketeers to ask, I have a feeling that flight by rocket is even more like this than flight by air. We are always going to find, the faster we go, the less we seem to be going fast. The more we do, the less we seem to be working.

The more nearly perfect physical activity becomes, the more it resembles mental activity. The more nearly perfect mental activity becomes, the more it resembles spiritual activity.

When we make a perfect prayer, we soar, as it were, free—released from bonds and bounds, in a world without obstructions, for we have risen higher than they extend.

We have become the bird that flies without having to move its wings, soaring serene on the upsweeping power that is the ever-rising spirit of life.

At our best, I suppose, we should pray to be like the saint who was so God-filled that God told him he could have any wish he asked.

The saint thought for a while and said, "Whenever, wherever my shadow falls behind me, may whatever it touches be blessed."

To make even our shadow falling unbeknownst behind us a prayer—could we wish for a greater joy than this? To be so much a part of life, so attuned to life, so much life's vessel, that life would flow through us unconsciously and naturally, without our taking thought! Life would flow through us and take root wherever it touched, spring up wherever it touched, flower wherever it touched.

And we would find our fulfillment not in the rewards of our

work but in the work itself, in doing what we are inspired to do, in being what we are formed to be!

Oh, what a way of life this would be!

Can a branch ask for more than this—that the life sap well up through it? And did the Master not tell you that you are a branch of the one vine?

Shall the branch cry to the tree, "Crown me with a crown. Give me a bag of money. Grant me honor and riches."

Or shall the branch cry, "Stir me with life. Send the life force through me. Let me live and be and grow."

So this is my prayer:

I say to my eyes, See.

I say to my ears, Hear.

I say to my voice, Speak.

I say to my mind, Think.

Feet, bear me up.

Heart, bear me forward.

Hands, perform.

And I say to myself, Live.

Live to the full tide of living.

⮜ A high-seas kind of life ⮞

Life is for the high seas. Let us live a high-seas kind of life. I am the human mariner for God.

I was meant for more than shallows.

I do not mean that we have to live a life of derring-do and danger to live at the full. We just have to live at the full.

Life at the full may be danger and derring-do. It may be hardship and pain. Or it may be safety and shelter. It may be peace and prosperity.

It may be plunging into a wilderness—of mind or of space.

It may be quietly cultivating a walled garden—outside your house or inside your soul.

There are high seas in the mind.

There are high seas in the heart. You need not go outside the room you sit in as you read this book—and you can be at the crest of living.

Right around you is a world as unexplored, as strange, as wonder-filled, as terror-filled, as glory-filled as all earth's distant untracked oceans.

Light streams from every atom. Power thunders from every crack of space. Life presses from every seed. Truth struggles to be released from every moment. Every moment new discoveries press and jostle one another, waiting for someone to reach out and seize them—no further away than a thought.

We live at the crest when we let life use us, when we dare to be ourselves and follow the bent of our soul.

Then we learn how natural it is to live at the crest.

Then we do not force; we let. We rise and fall with the waves of life; we ebb and flow with the tide; we accept the calms and bear the storms; we find it pleasant to ride sails furled at anchor; we find it pleasant also to crowd on every inch of sail and give ourselves to the wind that blows out of the deep!

We live naturally, easily, breathing in, breathing out, laying hold, giving forth, without taking thought—a creature-of-life and a life-creator.

We may not be free from terror, but we go forward; we may not be free from pain, but we work on. We may fail, but also we achieve. We may go down, but not before we have risen up.

Ours then becomes not a stingy, stinted existence, but large, free, generous, overflowing, exuberant life.

Let us pray to be not so much God-conscious as God-used.

Let me be your feet, God, and carry you wherever you direct me. And let me not be your feet because I think importantly, "Oh, it is God I am carrying!" Let my feet go where they go because they would bring comfort for suffering, and joy for sorrow, and food for hunger; and for the discouraged, faith in life.

Let me be your eyes, God. Let me never stop looking for beauty and pointing it out to others.

Let me be your voice, God. Let me never stop speaking truths.

Let me be your hands, God. Let me never stop doing loving acts for other human beings.

Lord, I would be alive!

Stretch me to the limit of my stretching; not so that I may have more of God, but so that I may give more of God.

We were not meant for sailing up and down a charted coast,

where every reef and shoal is curbed by a careful buoy. Beyond the cape, the high seas of the soul beat passionate and proud and undismayed.

Come, men! Come, mariners! Come, God's companions all!

IX

A CREATIVE POWER DOES THE WORK

❧ How did you turn it off? ❧

I said to the Master,
"How do I turn on the power of God?"
The Master said,
"How did you turn it off?"
Then I saw that if the power of God should be turned off even for a moment, the universe would crash to an end and crumble into nothingness.

The power of God is at work in every atom.
The power of God is at work in every mind.
The power of God is at work in you.

Night and day, pouring forth power, sending power surging through every trembling wire, the dynamos are at work in a city, whether the city wakes or sleeps.

Night and day, the power of God is at work, whether you turn it on or not. Whether you are awake to it or not, whether you know it or not, whether you invite it or not, the power is at work.

And it is at work in you.

You can refuse to use the power consciously—that is all.

But always, when you refuse to use the power consciously, the power may unconsciously use you.

The power of God presses at every point of being, waiting to be drawn forth.

How do you draw it forth?

Is not the best way to let it draw you forth?

For you can use the power of God to the extent of your capacity, but God uses you to the extent of His capacity.

Your wisdom is limited but God's wisdom has no limits.

So when you let God use you as He finds good, who can foresee what good will be brought forth?

Lightning and sunlight

The power that heals, the power that prospers, the power that solves problems, that turns inharmony into harmony and sorrow into joy, is a creative power. It is the creative energy of life. It is the creative energy of God.

It would be good if the creative power could be like the shining of the sun. I am sure that is the way it is meant to be with life, like sunlight.

For the sun—gentle, warm, life-giving—shines all the time. The creative energy flows steadily from the central source. All we have to do is turn toward it as the earth turns, out of darkness into light.

But at man's present level of development, getting the creative power to work is more like getting the lightning to shine than the sun.

Lightning hardly ever shines in a calm, unclouded sky. Often, only out of darkness, tumult, storm—out of agony of spirit and even of the flesh—do we get the bolt of creativity to flash.

Even then we cannot make it flash. We labor—and if we are fortunate, it flashes.

The thunderbolt—creative power—belongs to God.

We create the conditions in which God's light is most likely to shine forth. But God gives the light.

One day—I am certain—we will learn to abide in the light, as the earth abides in the light of the sun.

Perhaps, even some day as the sun abides in its own light.

That is why we must study the methods of prayer.

That is why we must practice meditation.

There is an art, even a science of prayer.

Yet more, there is a life of prayer.

The more we live this life, the closer we come to the time when the creative energy of God will pour through us freely, steadily, constantly as productive work.

How do I get a song to sing?

I cannot make creative things happen. But I can prepare for creative things to happen.

I can do what I can do.

I am a singer of songs. How do I get a new song to sing for me?

A song sings itself out of a singing spirit. A song sings itself out of a yearning need to sing. A song sings itself out of the music of being.

I cannot make a song sing itself.

I may draw it forth.

But I draw it forth the way a fisherman draws forth the fish of the sea. I cast in my nets and I wait.

That is the way it is with the power of God.

Rites may help. Prayers may help. Following rules may help. But they do not make the power of God work.

Only God can turn on the power of God.

I cannot make an apple germinate. But I can plant a seed. I can give it the warmth and light and water it needs. The seed may germinate; in season blossoms may appear; and the life force may give me even the golden apple of my desires.

I cannot make it rain the golden rain of God's ideas.

But I can dig ditches. I can study the laws that govern precipitation. I can learn what forces are at work to make the weather what it is. I can do all I can to set these forces in motion, to produce the conditions on which rain depends.

I can seed the clouds of life.

With what?

With faith.

With prayer.

With the expectation of good.

I can produce in myself the climate out of which answered prayer is likely to come.

Only God may answer prayer, but I can pray. I can establish the conditions on which answered prayer depends.

I can expect the good.

I can think positively.

I can affirm my oneness with the good.
I can accept the good when it appears.
I can lift up my mind.
I can sing praises to my God.
What is good?
Surely, to love is good.
To be creative is good.
To teach, to heal, to bring joy to others is good.
To turn the wilderness into a garden is good.
To look for a truth is good.
To make things beautiful and to make beautiful things is good.
To help men surpass themselves is good.

❧ Not to change God ☙

You do not pray to change God.
How would you change Him?
God is good.
He is your good.
Would you pray that He would become something other than that?

Whatever you conceive God to be, can you conceive Him to be less than good? More than good, perhaps. Beyond your highest concept of good. But not less than that. God is the always more.

Do you conceive of God as a harsh father? If you beg Him and beg Him, He may yield to your beggings.

Do you conceive of Him as your mother, a woman of whims? Keep asking, and you may catch her when she will let you.

God is not a man or woman like you—to be coaxed or moved by tears—to be entreated or cajoled or threatened.

If you think of God and what He is like, what words come to you?

I cannot believe you think of Him as something subject to whim or change.

Changeless may be one word.
Law may be one word.
Eternal may be one word.

Even if you think of Him as some mysterious kind of super-person, surely He is more than personal, not less.

Surely you do not see Him as a person moved by begging and entreating, changeable of mind. You see Him as a person, absolute in wisdom, seeing beyond question what is for your good, already bending to you in perfect love, holding you, as it were, next His heart and in His hand.

Would you change this?

There is only one way you could change God. That is to be less than love.

Less than wisdom.

Less than good.

For Love, Wisdom, Good—if He is anything—this He already is.

The purpose of prayer is to bring you into conformity with the laws of the universe so that the everlasting power and mercy may flow into you and through you.

I am such a little crab as lives in a salt-water pool by the sea. Should my little private pool of sea dry up, I do not sit on my haunches and beg the sea to come to me. I rise and go to the sea and unite myself with it—and I find that the sea has an everlasting supply of salt-water pools.

What can Life do except will life to those who turn to it?

And Love, will Love give less than the best it has to give to those who reach their hands to it?

Will Intelligence not try with all its power to bring forth light?

Will Power not try with all its skill to build and create?

God is life and love and intelligence and power.

Will He will less than these?

Will Life will death unless it leads to more life? Will Love will pain unless it leads to greater love?

We live in infinity, and it presses on me its infinite riches. But all I can take is what I can hold in my hands. Not a grain more.

There is a limitless supply of water in the reservoir, but no more gets into my cup than my cup can hold.

Infinity does not have to become more infinite. The reservoir does not have to be enlarged.

My capacity has to be enlarged.

God does not have to be changed. I have to be changed.

The everlasting rivers rush to fill the well, but I have to dig the well.

To pray is to dig the well.

✺ To contact a higher power ✺

Why do we pray?

We pray to contact a higher power or powers than we ordinarily have access to.

You may call this power God. You may think of it as many gods or spiritual beings. You may not think of it as any God at all.

You may feel that this power is wholly other than yourself. You may feel that this power is yourself.

You may think of this power as beyond. You may think of this power as within.

You may think of this power as dwelling in a faraway heaven. You may think of this power as inmost in your own nature.

How you think about the power you are trying to contact will make a difference in the kind of prayer you use.

But it will not change your purpose in praying.

For your purpose in praying is to quicken into activity the creative processes that lie at the root of being and out of which the world takes shape.

A tree grows from its roots upward.

A tree grows from its leaves downward.

Hesitantly, tremblingly, yet boldly and firmly, a tree thrusts its roots down into invisible, limitless deeps.

Hesitantly, tremblingly, yet boldly and firmly, a tree extends its leaves up into invisible, limitless deeps.

A tree gives itself to the unknown, at its root-tips, at its leaf-tips—and touches life and draws on life and expresses life.

Exploring, trusting, unfolding, assimilating, a tree grows, takes shape, and becomes what it is to become.

So it is with me.

I grow from within out.

Up from depths deeper than I understand a stream of life force wells.

Down from heights higher than I comprehend a rain of life force falls.

Prayer is a way of reaching up—to forces higher than my own.

Prayer is a way of reaching down—to forces deeper than my own.

I would grow and change.

I would change myself.

I would change my world.

I would grow to have more power, more wisdom, more love, more life.

I would do all I can to quicken the forces on which this growth and change depend.

This is why I pray.

Prayer puts me in order so that the life force may be used by me more effectively, so that the life force can flow through me without hindrance, freely, exuberantly. Then I breathe in living thoughts and breathe out happy acts.

I am like the ladder on which Jacob saw the angels going up and coming down out of heaven. When I am right with myself and in order, there is perfect movement from my inner world to my outer world and from the outer world to the inner world.

Life gives itself to me without holding back and I give myself to life without holding back.

Through me the life force expresses itself, and I express myself through the life force.

X

THE PRAYER OF SUBMISSION

⇜ *Here am I, Lord* ⇝

I said to the Master,
"To get God to do what I want Him to do, what do I have to do?"

"It is very simple," said the Master. "You follow the law of reciprocity.

"You do what God wants you to do; then, you find that God is doing what you want Him to do."

Then I saw that in order for the greater to become more, the smaller must be made to be less.

The way to become the master is to become the servant. The way to govern is to be governed.

There is a prayer of submission.

Isaiah made the prayer of submission when he said, "Here am I, Lord. Send me."

Have you ever tried to say these words and mean them?

There are no words harder to say.

Most of us, if we can say these words at all, say them reluctantly and with reservation.

"Send us, Lord—but not too far!"

When God comes and nudges us and whispers in our soul, "Whom shall we send, and who will go for us?" most of us, like Augustine, mutter irritably, "Presently Lord, presently."

It is recorded that Jesus Himself when at last he prayed the prayer, "Nevertheless not my will but thine be done," prayed in agony and "his sweat was as it were great drops of blood falling down to the ground."

The prayer of submission is a powerful prayer. It aligns us

with the Will of the Universe, with the Will that works at the root and core of life.

There is a Will that seeks to express itself.

It sends down roots and sends up stems and leaves.

It turns dust and gas into stars, and stars into living creatures.

It is life growing always more alive.

It is love becoming ever more loving.

It is intelligence thinking ever larger thoughts.

It is power raising its productive capacity to a higher power.

It is joy finding new levels of joy.

I cut myself. To the wound, where invading bacteria pour in, rushes a lonely phagocyte. There, at the farthest outpost of his world, he battles the invaders. I wonder if he cries out, "Help! Help!" and I wonder if he hears any answer.

He has an answer. For with all my might I dispatch to his aid all the forces of my being.

He gives himself that I may live. He serves my will.

I doubt that he ever understands what he is serving. I am another order of being, unlike anything he can possibly conceive. I am more than he can conceive; but because I am, he is more than he can conceive. Struggling there at the end of his world, alone to his thinking, and borne down at last in death, he serves a purpose higher than his highest dream.

Yes, even the ignoblest act of the human being he dies for is of an order nobler than his noblest hope. Is there any higher purpose than this—to give oneself for something more than oneself?

I would serve you, O Life.

I would give myself to you.

Are your purposes inscrutable?

As far beyond me as a poem or lovemaking or a rocket to the moon is beyond one of the cells in my body?

Then I would serve your inscrutable purposes.

Hold up your light, Life. Let it shine on my path that I may know what way to go, for when I go by your light I can only go toward more life.

⋖§ To accept, to consent §⋗

The Divine Will is good.

Its voice cries only and always: "More life, more love, more light!"

It works for order and it works for good.

It is always working to bring forth life.

It is always working to bring forth joy.

To submit is not to submit to suffering, to limitation. Submission may be life-affirming as well as life-denying.

To submit is to accept, to acquiesce, to consent.

But we can submit to light as well as to darkness. We can say yes to joy as well as to woe. We can submit to life.

To submit to life is to acquiesce in life, to consent to live.

To submit to life is to say that life is lord and love is lord, and we consent to do their sovereign will.

To submit to life is to trust in the goodness of life, and to have faith that when we do life's will we shall not be less alive, but more alive.

Mahomet submitted to life and brought forth man's most militant faith. He called his faith Islam, which means submission; He told his followers to call themselves Moslems, which means submitters. These submitters, an ignorant and backward band of half-wild nomads living at the edge of the known world, conquered the largest, continuous land-empire the earth has ever seen—it stretched at last from the Indonesian archipelago clear across Africa across the Straits of Gibraltar and up across Spain. They revived art and science and literature from the dark-age doldrums. They founded a religion that fourteen hundred years later is attracting more new believers than any other religion in the modern world.

Socrates submitted to the edicts of his neighbors, drank the hemlock, and died. Twenty-five hundred years later he is still the exemplar of the truth-seeker and of intellectual honesty for the Western world.

Jesus submitted and suffered crucifixion. Two thousand years later he is the greatest single influence on thought and on life that man has ever known.

We can submit to the factors that defeat us. But we can also submit to the factors that lead us to victory.

To submit is to follow the way. The way leads always to life. For it is the way of my own being.

When I make Love the master of my fate and Intelligence the captain of my soul, I submit to the highest and the best in my own nature and to the highest and the best in the universe.

I cry out, "Love, You are my Lord. Use me. Wisdom, You are my teacher. Teach me.

"Here is my stubborn heart. Soften it, Love; take it and make it yours.

"Here is my unseeing mind. Show it the way to go, Spirit of Light. Guide it in the way that it can use its powers for the good of my fellows."

Why did you choose?

All of us submit.

But to what do we submit?

Of the important things in your life, how many have been of your making? How many have been of life's making?

Of the important things in your life, about how many of them can you tell me, "This is of my conscious choosing"?

And of these, about how many of them can you tell me, "This is why I chose"?

Did you choose the city of your birth? Or your parents? Or your children?

Do you like to read a book like this? I hope so. Why do you prefer this to watching a football game? Or, why would you rather watch a football game than read a book? Do you like to play chess better than golf or would you rather dance?

Do you like to eat fish? Or apple pie? Can you tell me why?

Do you like blondes better than brunettes—or is it the other way?

Are you a mechanic? A salesman? A teacher? A bookkeeper? Or a businessman? Can you tell me why?

Why do you live in the city where you live?

I am not saying that you can give me no answers to any of these questions. But at best you can give me only partial answers, never complete, and to many you can give me no answer at all.

You like blondes and football and the West Coast. That is all. You are a salesman and have a wife and two children, one boy, one girl. You catch cold easily and once in a while drink too much beer. As to why all this is true, it might take a book to explain. Or a psychoanalyst. Or better, a seer. It is just the way you are. That is all.

We all submit—to inward drives and to outer necessities.

We bow to this and not that, and follow the imperatives of our being without heed or question.

But when we submit to life—to love and intelligence—we follow only the highest and best in us, and we let ourselves be used—not idly and meaninglessly, but for the high purposes of life.

We submit, whether consciously or unconsciously. We acquiesce willingly, or are blindly driven. We go as the slave of circumstance —or child of the King.

But when we know what we are submitting to, when we say boldly and freely, "I choose to serve life and to give myself to life," then life does not thrust us headlong down blind alleys, but leads us along the highway of self-realization.

All of us—the wisest, the most learned, the most spiritual— walk an unknown way.

We may walk as by night, stumblingly, from dark into dark. Or we may put our hand in love's hand and go forward. We may look to the light that life holds up for us, and walk on.

When we do this, the way may bring us gratification or it may ask of us renunciation, but it is always a way of self-realization.

It never leads to less, always to more. If it seems to lead to less, it is only that the lesser should decrease so that the greater may increase.

❧ One syllable at a time ❧

God does not have to come to us before we go to Him.

We have read the famous stories—how the Lord appeared to

Saul on the road to Damascus; how the angel Gabriel came to Mahomet in a cave; how Augustine was converted as he prayed in a garden; how the Buddha found enlightenment as he sat under a fig tree.

Someone may have told us, "You have to be converted."

We may have read in religious literature how the Holy Spirit comes down in tongues of flame.

We may have gone to a revival meeting and seen people caught up in religious ecstasy and heard them talking in tongues.

But the Spirit of God is not a once-in-a-lifetime something that appears to us as a peculiar emotional-mystical experience, a kind of psychic seizure, and never appears to us again.

If God is ever with us, He is with us always. He is incessantly, everlastingly with us—incessantly, everlastingly at us.

I am sure there are times when he shouts at us, shakes us, even kicks us, but only when we are very obstinate. Most of the time He is nudging us gently and whispering quietly in our ear. This He never ceases to do. We may pay no attention, His is such a still small voice—but we hear. We may not move in the direction He points out to us, for His light is just a thought in our own mind—but we know the way is there.

Most of the time all of us—even the Pauls and Augustines and Mahomets and Buddhas—move a step at a time, and not by mighty leaps upward. We only take a mighty leap upward because we have come a step at a time to the point where a mighty leap upward is the next step to take.

God comes as surely to the man writing a book—or to the man reading one—as He does to the person who suddenly falls prostrate at the revival meeting and babbles incoherently.

What a disordered world this would be if it were not so!

Life reveals its truths to us dramatically, with all its trumpets blowing, but most of the time it just whispers them in our mind one syllable at a time.

It is like the way spring comes back after winter. Suddenly one day we look and it is green. But the green came back one cell at a time at the growing tip of the world.

That is the way growth comes. We grow so slowly we cannot see that we are growing—we can only see that we have grown.

~§ A *sense of direction* §~

Once I was talking with friends about the Holy Spirit and conversion.

One asked, "What is conversion?"

Another answered, "A conversion is the resolution of conflict."

The resolution of conflict!

I liked that, and I still do.

For this takes the religious experience out of the occasional and the strange and makes it what it ought to be if it is going to be valuable—part of daily experience.

Another way to say it might be, "Conversion is finding a right sense of values."

Once I know what gold is, will I not weigh all substances by it to find their worth!

I want my God to be the wonderfully strange and strangely wonderful. I want Him to be extraordinary experiences—and because He is infinite He will be.

But if He is to have meaning for me, if He is to be something I live by and for and through, then He must appear to me in ordinary, daily ways. He must be the voice of reason and the impulse of love. He must be my own best thought and the generous impulse in my own heart. He must be the inclination of my own highest nature.

He must speak to me in English—if He wishes me to answer. He must come to me as inward need and outward circumstance— if He would have me go His way.

For as thought and impulse and circumstance, He is always present, and not once in a lifetime.

And this is how I need Him—as an instant and a constant help.

I have laid hold of the Holy Spirit, I have been converted, I have found God—when I have found a right sense of values. This does not mean that I have reached the goal.

But it does mean that I know where I want to go. I have not arrived, but I have set out on the journey; I am no longer an aimless wanderer.

To him who has no harbor he is making for, no wind is the right wind. But when we know where we want to go, every passing breeze can help us on our way.

Ho there, little sailorman, adrift in your cockle shell of self, alone upon an endless ocean, whirled round by every turning wind and tossing wave, not knowing where the shore may be, not knowing whether you are being driven toward land or farther out to sea—what would you give for a light? What would you give for a sign of direction?

When you have said to God—whatever you may conceive Him to be—"Thou, Lord!" you have a sense of direction.

You are going in His direction.

The wind of His love blows steady all the time. Set your sail. His love will carry you across the widest, wildest sea.

☙ The way of attunement ❧

There is a way to get the power of God to do what we want it to do; to heal us when we need healing; to supply our needs when we feel lack; to comfort us when we are troubled; to bring us friends when we are lonely, joy for grief and peace for pain; to light our path when we are lost and wander frightened in the dark.

It is the way that a rainbow is made after rain. It is the way that morning is made to follow night and spring is made to come after winter.

It is the way that a bare branch brings forth green leaves.

It is the way that the mist rises out of the sea, and the way that an ugly waterbug changes into a dragonfly.

Do you know this way?

It is the way of attunement.

It is the way of being one with the way of things.

At the core of being is a rhythm; when you place yourself in tune with this cosmic rhythm, all things work together for you and you work in harmony with all things.

There is a way of things. That is all you can say of it.

But learn the way of things and follow the way—walk in the way, work in the way—and everything will go your way.

The universe is God's work. He made it very good. He made it to bring forth good. He made it to move and grow, to unfold and expand. When you move with the universe, the universe moves with you—and through you and for you.

Then there is nothing you cannot do or be because all the forces of the universe—all the expanding energies of life—are focused in you and pour through you to come into expression.

The miracle-worker—whether you call him scientist or saint, or son of God—is always the man who learns the way of things and lives in accord with it.

He recognizes the power that is there; he studies it until he sees how it works; then he works with it—and it works through him. He lifts his hand; he utters the word—and the power rushes forth!

Then the rest of us stand round and gaze open-mouthed in awe, beholding the healing, or the thunderbolt; the light for our house, or for our mind; the turning wheels, or the overturned world; the life where no life was expected to be!

Set your will against the will of the way of things, and the Supreme Will will hurl you down against yourself, a tiny, shivering, impotent islet of lonely self-ness.

But walk in the way and work with its will, and you will find that the Supreme Will is working only to fulfill the dearest desires of your heart.

Like King Canute, you can wade into the sea and forbid the rising tide to rise. The tide, unheeding of your paltry crown, will tumble you into the waves.

But make yourself a channel through which the power of the tide may express itself; study how the tide works and do what you have to do to let it work through you—and the tide will do all your work for you.

What gift will it not come bringing you? It will make you not a little King Canute, but serve you as a son of the King of Kings.

When we learn how the tide turns, we learn that it turns for us. Let it turn as it will, and it will take you where you will.

When we learn how the wind blows, we learn that it blows for us. Let it blow as it will, and it will take you where you will.

Learn to tack with the wind.

Learn to veer with the tide.

The wind and tide will take you wherever you want to go.

A *wind* and *a tide*

Do not settle for little dreams.

You are yourself the dream of Him who dreamed the sun and stars.

And He meant you for more.

That is why you hear forever the cry for more in your flesh.

That is why you cannot be content with littleness; you can accept it, but you cannot be content.

The flowers in your garden open and close.

The birds fly south in autumn and north again in spring.

The earth spins shining around the sun, singing psalms of day and night.

The sun and all the stars breathe in and out and ebb and flow to winds and tides of a sea too vast for our imagining.

Listen.

Be still.

Then, perhaps, if you are still enough, you can hear the everlasting tide of being flinging itself on the shore of forever. The tides that run in all earth's oceans are mere ripples in a pond compared to this tide.

And it pulses for you.

Perhaps, if you are still enough, you can hear the universe breathing in and breathing out again. All the winds that sweep earth's ocean of air—zephyrs and breezes and gales and hurricanes —are like a child's blowing of bubbles compared to this breath.

And it breathes for you.

There is a wind that blows over the world.

There is a tide that moves the world of space and all the worlds beyond the world of space.

This wind, I think, is the breath of God, and this tide is the pulsing of His heart.

✌ Made for soul-faring ⧚

The winds and the waves of God's sea are high and have no end.

Look where you will, the seas stretch yet beyond.

Do you wonder how we shall find our way in such a sea?

Do not be afraid.

Seafarers all, we came hither in a ship no man remembers, by a course no man can chart on any map. Not by sails our ship was driven over this sea, nor with oars, nor on wings like a ship of the air. For this deep, from which we drew, is deeper than space. All the worlds of space are but an island in this ocean.

Yet it is no unfamiliar deep; nor are its courses unknown, though they are uncharted.

Its mysteries are graven in our inmost self. Without remembering, we know its ways as the migratory plover knows its way through the trackless air. No one has to tell us how to go, as no one has to tell the salmon or the eel. No star need shine in the sky for us to reckon our course by. Our light is in ourself.

There will be tempests, but we are stronger than tempest—and the calm is in our soul, not in the sea.

There will be night, but we are children of the light.

We were meant for the deep, not for the shallows. We came out of it. We return into it. It is our native element, a spiritual dimension. We are spiritual beings and were made for soul-faring.

Separated from the sea, we are soon no more than an empty shell on a windy dune. But the sea comes to the conch of our soul, singing the old songs, the ancient, ageless music, though to our ears the sounds seem ever a new and startling truth.

The seas of God come thundering over the reefs of space and the cliffs of time. The seas of God come thundering at the seawalls our heart has raised, thundering at the gates of thought.

We must open the gates and let the great seas in. For this is the water of life.

O heart of love, O breath of life, O everlasting One whose

dancing feet spin the heavens on their rhythmic round, we too pulse, breathe, and live in You.

The waves of Your thought roll, roll in our mind.

The winds of Your will blow, blow through our heart.

They will carry us to far shores and over trackless deeps. But they carry us to a fulfillment and a consummation greater even than our loveliest dream.

XI

PRAYING FOR THINGS

⊰ *Nothing can be possessed* ⊱

I said to the Master,

"Tell me about things. Is it wrong to pray for things?"

The Master said, "It is wrong not to pray for things. If prayer is right, then there is no aspect of living that we should not pray about.

"Pray about things, and you will find that you have the things you need, and you have also the attitude toward things you need."

Then I thought about things.

I saw that it is futile to pray for the possession of things, for things can never be possessed.

Nothing can be possessed. We have the use of things, but we never have the possession of them, however many titles to them we may deposit with the recorder of deeds, however many locks and strongboxes we may use for hiding them. There is nothing that is ours to keep. Not one thing. Sooner or later, we will have to give it away or it will be taken away. Everything. Even our body. Even our mind. Everything was the gift of life. And life asks it back. According to the greatest teacher of all, life asks it back with interest; life expects it to have grown under our care. Life asks what we have done with what was given us. Have we turned it into a trash heap, or into a park?

Life is for us to be alive in.

Life is not to build a castle on. A castle is a vast pile of stones, damp, gloomy, and usually uncomfortable. After a short time, nobody wants to live there any more; then it becomes a ruin.

Life is to grow a garden in. A garden lives. A garden grows. A garden changes a bare patch of land into a place of trees and flowers and grass and fountains splashing into pools and singing birds and buzzing insects.

Life is not a thing of stones for stones, but a thing alive for things alive—for May flies and pine trees and hummingbirds, and you and me.

A gardener knows what a garden is like. A gardener knows that no one possesses a garden.

No one owns the land. In a well-built house the landlord is merely a lodger—with rooms for a week, a year, five years, fifty years. Generations of mockingbirds sing in the branchtops. Generations of moles tunnel the lawns, smelling out the grubs that live here, too. The rabbits mock at the fences; the pokeweed lords it in the lot corner; the flower garden belongs no more to the gardener than to the bees that sup the flowers. In the limestone of the walls are the remains of shellfish that swam here once, and perhaps . . . the gardener is content to plant his trees and not trouble himself as to who will lie in their shade.

✑ Not for forever ‿

Till the ground, tend the plant, pluck the flower as you wish. But the garden grows with spring and rests with fall.

You may take the flower, dry it, and place it in a glass case— but it is not the flower. You have only a bit of colored straw, slowly fading, slowly powdering. Keep it long enough and you will have only colorless dust.

Things are not for forever.

Things are like smiles and frowns that flit across the face of the Eternal. When a smile becomes fixed, it turns into a grimace. When a frown becomes fixed, it is just another wrinkle.

To enjoy things is not to possess them or to be possessed by them, but to use them. The joy of anything is the use of it. The joy of anything is to take it and make it into something more.

Rows of dresses hanging dusty in a closet, dresses no one wears any longer; tools slowly rusting in a tool shed, where no one comes to work; books that have gotten yellow and brittle with age because no loving hand ever fondles them or opens their pages; or a house in which no one has lived for a long time— there are few things sadder than these.

The joy is not to have a shining plane in your tool chest,

but to take the plane out and plane a board with it until the
board is flat and smooth and true.

To do this is to know what things are for.

The joy is not to have a beautiful dress in your closet, but
to wear the dress to make the day or evening colorful and bright
and interesting to you and your friends—or even to give it away
when you will not wear it.

The joy is not to have a book upon a shelf, neat and perfect
in its shining clean dust jacket, but to read the book and rejoice
in its information or its inspiration, even to scribble in its
margin—or to lend it to friends to read, even friends who never
return it.

It is right to pray for things. When you pray, pray knowing
that life lavishes its things, crowding every crack of space with
its fecund living stuff, pressing into every outstretched hand its
overflowing bounty.

Know, too, that things are not for forever. Things are not to
hold on to. Hold on long enough and you will wish you had
cast even the dearest thing away.

There is a great Japanese myth. It is about twin deities, Izanagi
and Izanami, who were devoted lovers and produced the Japanese
islands and their people. When Izanami died in childbirth, the
sorrowing Izanagi could not let her go but followed her into the
underworld begging her to return to him. When he neared her
in the darkness, she asked him not to look at her, for she knew
that death had not made her sightly. But he lit the comb that
held his hair in place, and saw her moldering.

Clutch things to you, and when life comes round again, where
will it leave its gifts? For whatever you have, life has yet more to
give.

The snake must slough its skin; the bird must molt its feathers;
and the evergreen that lives for a thousand years must give up
many of its boughs as it grows.

Is the corn less because it gives itself for food?

Or the sun because it gives itself for light?

Things are made for life, not life for things. Pray for them,
knowing that they are yours to use, to enjoy, and to expend—for
the increase of your own joy-in-living and for the joy-in-life of
others.

⋐§ Not a single cell §⋑

Then I saw that my body does not belong to me, and never has. I have the use of it for a certain time, but in the end I must give it up, as I must give up house and land. I cannot keep it, not a single cell of it.

As a matter of fact, I have already given it up. For my body is not one thing but many. If I manage to live in it any time at all, I will have lived in many bodies in this one. For not a single cell of the body I was born with now remains.

I do not shed like a dog or molt like a bird; I do not cast off my shell all at once like a crab, or my skin like a snake; but cell by cell, invisibly, continually, I am tearing down the old structure and building it anew. I wonder how many times I have in this lifetime rebuilt this structure that I call my body, enlarging and narrowing, tearing out and adding on, altering and reshaping.

Life has not let me keep the body I was born with or the body I occupied when I was ten or twenty or thirty. I have had to move out of them all. I have torn them down and rebuilt them, until this lodging I now occupy bears little resemblance to those I formerly occupied.

Did you know me a quarter century ago, I doubt that you would recognize me if you met me today. If you remember me from half a century ago, I know you would not recognize me.

If I met myself of a century ago, I would not recognize that it was I.

How old are you? Twenty-five? Fifty? Seventy-five? What did you look like a hundred years ago? A thousand years ago? Ten thousand years ago? You who think of yourself in such fixed terms, what were you like then?

⋐§ A kind of landlord §⋑

I said to my Lord,

"Lord, I see that this body does not belong to me, and I have only the use of it for a little time. So I give it to you.

"You have given it to me, not to own, but to use.

"You are a kind of landlord. You move me into lodgings. And somehow I see that they are accommodations where I belong at the moment.

"But you will not let me stay in them for long. A few years at most, and you make them over again.

"You are not like some of the landlords I have known. You are always redecorating the house and rebuilding the fixtures. You are the renewing Spirit—you are life—and you are constantly making all things new.

"Ten years, at the most—and every brick, every board, every nail in the house has been replaced with a new one."

The Master Builder builds, and I have a sense that it is at my direction.

He works in secret but to specifications I provide—do not ask me how or where.

If the house is not to my liking, let me order a different one.

How?

Through my thinking, feeling, desiring. No other way.

The house is the one I ordered and fits my inmost wants and needs, however loudly I may complain about the plumbing or the furnace or the leaking roof.

Once a man bought the house next door to where I then lived.

Before he bought, he saw me working in my garden and came up to me.

"Can you tell me anything about this house?" he asked.

I said, "There is a spring in the basement. They built it over a spring."

Nevertheless, he bought the place. After a while, the water bubbled up through the basement floor and the walls buckled; whenever it rained, the house sat in a pool.

The man complained to the sellers, to me, and to the Lord.

How unjust things were!

Do not ask me why, but the man needed to live in a house with a spring in the basement.

And so do many of us!

We order the house the way it comes.

Here I am in this body, with the many excellencies and few flaws it happens to have.

The Builder is working away this moment, changing the walls here, plastering the ceiling there, taking out worn bricks and boards and putting new ones in.

And somehow I think he is doing it to suit me, to provide what I really want and need.

Though I am not aware of having given the orders, I think the house is what I made it to be.

If the plumbing does not work as it should or a wall is askew, the builder built to blueprints that my secret soul provided.

Listen! The builder is building even now. Right this moment he is making alterations. It is not too late to change the plans.

⋖§ Body and mind §⋗

There is a sense in which your body is only a thing.

Your mind is only a thing.

What have you done with your body? Have you used it to the fullest? Have you run as fast as you can run and leaped as far as you can leap? Have you danced with grace and agility? Have you sung at the top of your voice?

Have you expressed all that your body has to express, pressed it to its utmost and beyond?

Have you ever set your mind free and followed where it led— not down known ways and familiar paths but into country where no paths appear, where you yourself must find the path and mark the way?

Have you never given your mind problems that it could not answer?

For you have this body and this mind for a few years or for many years.

And even this misstates the truth.

For this is not the body you were born with, nor is this the mind you were born with.

Of the body you were born with, not a single atom remains in the body that is yours to use now.

And the mind you were born with—what have you done with that? What new powers have you given it? In what new directions have you sent it? What has it grown to become?

When you pray for things, pray knowing that things are not for forever—not even your body, not even your mind.

⌣§ *Truth, beauty, love, life* §⌣

Truth, beauty, love, life—these are for forever. But that is only because you never have them, but only the shadow of them. You have them darkly as in a mirror.

You hear truth like a music; like a horn that sounds from a far-off hill. And you follow, you follow. But beyond each far horizon, there are new horizons still—and beyond the last horizon, truth calling like a horn.

You see beauty like a vision, like a dream that wakes you in the night, full of longing, full of a sense of imminent perfection; but it fades. You try to remember the dream and to put down what you remember. But the beauty you lay hold of is only an elusive reflection of the beauty you envision.

You feel love, like a handclasp, like the touch of lips. You feel its warmth and joy, and you know that it alone gives meaning to life. But when you seek to possess love and keep it for yourself, it slips from your embrace. You must loose it and let it go. For love is not something you can keep, but only something you can give. And you have it only by giving it away.

And life—what about life?

Life is the flower that you can have only as long as you do not pluck it.

Life is the fruit that you can have only as long as you leave it on the tree.

Life is alive.

It changes.

It grows.

It is yours to live, not to possess.

Once a Chinese artist, laboring for seven years, carved out of jade a mulberry leaf so perfect that when it was placed among real mulberry leaves, no one could tell which was which.

When it was shown to the Emperor, he only said: "How fortunate we are that it does not take Nature so long!"

And indeed, though for a short time it might fool my careless eyes, how long would the leaf fool a silkworm—or a mulberry tree!

For a real mulberry leaf, green and growing or fading and falling, has a power to give life—yes, even though it falls forgotten into the leafy womb of autumn—that the poor little perfect jade leaf can never have!

And persons?

What is a person?

Certainly not a thing.

But you cannot have a person forever any more than you can have a thing forever.

When you pray for persons and about persons, you must bear in mind that you can never possess another person, not even as much as you can a flower.

For a person is a flower—the human flower of God!

XII

PRAYING FOR OTHERS

⋙ When God has been there ⋘

Then I said to the Master, "How shall I pray for another?"

The Master said, "Before you can pray for another, you must first pray for yourself."

I thought about the many times I have prayed for others. I saw that I have never prayed for another and received a good report about the results of my prayers when I did not myself feel lifted up and moved. I was changed. I was touched. The power of God had flashed in me.

Perhaps the person I was praying for was miles away, but I had a sense of something happening. Something was happening—in me. A change had occurred in me. Later I learned that a change had occurred in regard to the condition about which I had been praying, too.

When the woman touched the hem of Jesus' garment, He knew that something had gone out of Him. When the current flows through it, a wire—inanimate though it is—is touched and changed. It glows and is warm. How much more touched and changed is a man when God uses him to carry the current of His healing power!

I am myself as changed by praying for another as by praying for myself; I am as changed as the one I pray for—not in the same way, but as much.

God—or life—cannot use me without changing me.

This is because it is the power of God—or life—that brings about the answer to prayer. It is not through my power that prayer is answered but through God's.

The power of God flows through me. The power of God uses

me. I am only needed to make contact. But God—or life—cannot use me without changing me.

We always know when God has been there. We find His footprint, as it were, where he has gone by. Where His hand touches earth, flowers spring forth, flowers of the spirit, life, love, light—a child, a poem, a healing, an answered prayer.

When God is there, something changes. Either we change or conditions change. A light comes on. Power is conveyed. Beauty rushes forth. Joy bursts into being.

God is never there without leaving His mark. Perhaps it is a word. Perhaps it is an idea. Perhaps it is a quickened spirit. Perhaps it is a poem. Perhaps it is a renewed life. Perhaps it is an answered prayer.

No matter how long I pray, I rarely have a sense of contact with God for more than a few moments. Sometimes I think that we can stand contact with God only for moments—but that moment is enough to change us, it is enough to change the world.

It is like digging a well and drinking water.

Though the river we tap be infinity itself, how much can we drink? A cupful? Two cupfuls? We can hold no more.

ᴈ§ The wire, the light, and the power §ᴈ

The whole purpose of my prayers—whether I pray for myself or someone else—is to unify myself with God, with the Creative Spirit.

We have a wrong notion of the role of thought in prayer when we think we send out thoughts to others when we pray for them.

When I pray for you, I do not help you through the power of my powerful thoughts. I have no power to change you. I have no power to change God. I have only the power to change myself. This is all I can do. But this is all I have to do.

I am God's wire. I do not have to tell God's power where to go; God knows where He is needed. I do not have to direct Him. I only have to carry the power.

I have to give Him myself for His love and power to flow through. God does the work, but He does it through me.

I reach out—toward the power. I reach out—toward the light.

It is not my thoughts that heal and bless. To think this is for an electric wire to think that it is the power that lights the room. The wire is neither the light nor the power. All the wire does is provide contact.

By taking thought, I make myself a receptacle that the power can flow through. By taking thought, I establish the conditions in which the answer to prayer can flash forth. By taking thought, I create a climate in which the creative act can take place.

The climate is the same whether I am praying for myself or someone else. The same conditions are necessary; the same work has to be done by me, and the same power—the creative power of Spirit—is at work.

I have to work on my thoughts when I pray—not so that I can send them to another human being, but to get them right with God.

The role of thought is to get me right with God. The role of thought is to create the climate in which the creative act may take place.

All I can do to help myself or you is to get myself right with the creative forces of the universe. When I have the right perspective toward me, when I am in my right place, the power of God may pour through me to bless—you, if you reach!

It is as when I am working with a balky machine and bless it with a thought of order. The thought of order is most of all for me. When I am in order, when I have established my right relationship with God and with the things in my world, everything is in order.

I seek and find the spring, that is all. I draw the water and fill the cup. I hold it out—for everyone who comes that way.

And you—you do not have to drink. When you are thirsty enough, you will.

◦§ *My own mind's shield* §◦

I have prayed and counseled with others for many years. When people tell me about influencing others through their thoughts, I always wonder what kind of strange people they have been praying with—or what kind of strange people I have been praying with.

One thing the people I have counseled with have never done is to accept my thoughts. I have almost only to suggest that something is the case to have the person I am working with resist that thought and never accept it. I have to be very careful to get people to see things for themselves, even when what I would point out to them is obviously the truth.

I have found people to guard their minds jealously and to resist the intrusion of thoughts anyone tries to plant there.

Am I to believe, then, that God has made us so resistant to the suggestions of others, when they are consciously given—even when they are true and right and helpful—but has left us vulnerable to the suggestions of others, when the thoughts are sent to us silently and unconsciously? It is hardly likely.

I happen to believe in telepathic communication. I am certain it occurs.

But I believe no less certainly that God has given me the right to determine my own life. The world is no doubt full of thought as it is full of radiation. But somehow I carry my own mind's shield.

It is almost as if my mind, like my body, has a built-in immunity reaction, so that it accepts only what is its own. Certainly only those thoughts I open the door to, get in. No one can influence me by his thought against my will—no matter how well intentioned he is; no matter how much of a do-gooder he is; no matter how much he wants to help.

Love can help me, because there is no shield against love. Life can help me, because I am a leaf on the tree of life. God can help me, because He and I are one.

ᜍᜓ A steed named "Cloud" ᜉᜓ

The Buddhists sometimes represent the savior as a winged steed named "Cloud," who soars through the skies above the ocean of life to rescue the shipwrecked.

In one story some sailors set out for the Island of Jewel. But on the way they stop on another island inhabited by beautiful and willing seductresses. Life is so gratifying here that they stay, although they find that the seductresses are sirens—man-eating monsters, who will consume them all. But from time to time Cloud appears above the island and cries out to the imperiled sailors that they may mount on his back if they will and be carried to the farther shore. In the story, they may not look back; if they do, they topple off into the sea.

But Cloud does not save these sailors by directing his thought toward them—except to be moved with compassion for them. Cloud saves them by perfecting his own powers of flight.

If we would save others from drowning, we had better learn how to swim.

In the end, the only way we will save them is by helping them to learn to swim for themselves. Sooner or later they are going to have to plunge into the stream and make the crossing. The time to begin swimming lessons, however, is not when we come on them sinking and crying for help. Let us hold them up and get them to the shore. Then we can hope that they will want to learn.

No one can grow for another. No one can live for another. No one can do what you have to do or be what you have to be, no matter how much he may love you or wish to help you. I may be able to solve a problem or two for you—though if I continue to solve your problems for you too long we may both wish we had stopped in time.

Even those whom Jesus healed all finally perished. Each man has to grow for himself and in himself.

We can help one another. That is why there are so many of us; we are not meant to live to ourselves alone—or for ourselves alone. And I do not believe we can. We are made for love. We are made to help one another.

But in the end the truest help you have to give is not to offer me your strength, but to help me to find my own strength; not to offer me your knowledge, but to help me to develop my own powers of thought; not to offer me your life, but to quicken in me the love and joy of life.

⤘ It is only love ⤙

How do you pray for someone you want to help?

First, reach out in your mind for God. You do not have to

reach far. He is right where you are. He is right where the one needing help is.

Work with your thought until you realize that God's perfection is—and it is everywhere. Think about the one you are helping and know that he is enveloped in God's perfection.

Every time your thought returns to him, return him in your thought to God.

See him perfect in your mind's eye, if you will.

Feel him perfect in your heart's love—this you must.

Prayer is an act of thought. But when we are praying for another, prayer is even more an act of love. For it is only love that makes us one with one another.

Love always has power. For love does not bind. Love does not command. Love does not possess. Love frees. Love always puts the happiness of the loved one before our own. Love gives itself. Love looks for no return. Love makes itself less so that the loved one may be more.

Love does not say, even secretly, "May it be as I wish it, or as I see it wise, or as I feel it to be good." Love says to each one, "May you follow the law of growth of your own being; may you be what your own uniqueness makes you to be." Love gives the loved one to life.

There is one prayer that always has power to help others. There is one prayer we can always make for another, whether he asks for prayer or not. This is the prayer of love. To make the prayer of love is to see the one for whom we are praying perfect in spite of flaws; for this is how love always beholds the beloved. When we do this, we call forth the highest and best in everyone for whom we pray.

I have been part of a very great prayer ministry for many, many years. This is the prayer ministry called Silent Unity. In Silent Unity a group of about one hundred persons pray for others who ask for prayer from all over the world. In Silent Unity prayer goes on night and day and has gone on continually, for almost a century. We in Silent Unity maintain this vigil of prayer in many different ways, but once a day we all meet together in a prayer room. Over the door of this prayer room one simple prayer is printed:

"I Behold the Christ in You."

It is a prayer I have uttered thousands of times. For it is the true prayer of love—to see another as faith sees him, as love sees him, as God sees him; to see through human appearances to the divine essence that abides at the central core of the being of every man.

⋅⋅⋅ The prayer that is love ⋅⋅⋅

I said to the Master,
"Tell me about the prayer that is love."
The Master said,
"Tell me about the prayer that is not love."
For if a prayer does not have love in it, how will it get to the heart of things?

And if a prayer does not get to the heart of things, how will it change what has to be changed?

For things can be destroyed from the outside in. But things can only grow from the inside out.

And prayer changes things by causing them to grow.

God makes contact with us through our heart—always there—in the unconscious deeps of our nature. It is in the heart, the unconscious deeps, where the creative act always takes place.

Here is the secret place of the Most High.

Here is the house of the creative Spirit of life.

Here is the mansion of miracles.

Here is where the Infinite finds finite expression.

Here is where man and God are linked.

Here at our heart we have only to step a prayer's length to be in the heart of God.

Here at our heart we have only to love to be in the heart of another.

But we have to love.

There is a secret room at the heart of being where all hearts have contact and are not separate but one.

But only love can enter that room.

And God is love.

Here there is no you and I. Here there is only love. Here if I be lifted up, I draw you upward with me.

For it is the God who is love that is lifted and it is the love that is God who lifts.

❧ Not for myself alone ❧

You can work without love and you can pray without love. But the work you do without love will have no joy in it and you will detest its products. The prayer you make without love will be a selfish prayer, and though it bring you ten thousand things, it will never bring you peace of mind or any lasting satisfaction.

There is a sense, of course, in which we cannot pray to God without praying in love, because God is love, and whenever we turn to Him we open ourselves to love, and love comes in, whether we will or not.

There is a sense in which any prayer is a prayer of love. For we cannot pray for ourself alone.

When we pray for anyone—even if it is ourself—we pray for everyone.

I cannot pray for myself without praying for my brother, and I cannot pray for my brother without praying for my enemy. For prayer is that which unites me with God, and the nearer I draw to God, the nearer I draw to my fellows.

Prayer breaks down the wall that separates me from God, but when I have broken down the wall, any man who happens by may pass through the opening I have made.

Prayer is the hand I extend to God. But when I extend my hand in prayer, then any man who comes along may lay hold of my outstretched hand and be drawn up with me.

Prayer never shuts anyone out. We may shut people out in our thought; we may even, in our foolishness and ignorance, pray to hurt others—but God—who is love—laughs at our childishness—and He makes of our cry of hate a psalm of love.

Prayer is the well I dig.

I may dig the well for myself.

But the well of God is an artesian well. It gushes with such force that it cannot be contained in my little bucket of self. It rushes across the earth in a stream, watering everything it touches, quenching the thirst of any man who comes and kneels to drink.

When I pray, I am like one who climbs into a tree when the fruit is ripe. Though I climb but to find an apple for myself, that I may bring down and eat alone, I cannot climb without shaking every limb of the tree so that many apples fall to earth, apples that any hungry man who passes by may carry away and eat.

How ripe and how abundant is the fruit of the tree of God! And God's love is a tree that grows in no man's private orchard, but by the public road where all men must pass by.

No man can pray to himself alone.

Are you thirsty? My prayer will give you drink.

Are you hungry? You may take of my prayer and sup.

✌ When a devil is loved ⧉

I saw the power that is in a prayer of love, for I saw a Man of love come to the gate of Hell.

There the devils waited for him with ugly instruments of pain—tongs and firebrands and seething filthy potions.

Naked and alone, he passed through the gate and went into that noisy, noisome land.

The devils, clambering, clamoring, swarmed round him to seize him.

But the Man was not looking at the snarling faces of the devils. He was looking at the anguished inhabitants of Hell running to and fro in writhing pain. And the Man's self went out to them in love and pity.

The Man was not listening to the screeching of the devils. He was hearing the screams of the tortured, and his heart went out to them in prayer and compassion.

The Man was not thinking of the devils at all. He was feeling the longing of the damned to escape from their suffering, and his mind lost itself in devising ways of helping them.

The devils rushed at the man with their tongs, but the tongs did not seize him.

They rained firebrands on him, but the fire did not burn him.

They spilled their seething filthy potions over his head, but the seething filth did not soil him.

Brushing through the swarms of spitting angry devils as if they were gnats or flies, the Man went to those who screamed and writhed and agonized.

Though his hands were empty and he stood naked before them and had no balm for their wounds save his love and no drink for their thirst save his pity, he gave them his love. He gave them his prayer. He gave them his thought. He spoke words of cheer. Where he found them fallen, he lifted them up. Where he could, he interposed himself between them and their tormentors.

Some thanked him. Some cursed him. But he did not give himself to them because of their curses or their thanks, but because he loved them.

And he loved the devils no less than those they bedeviled. For he saw that the torturers also were tortured, and the pain they inflicted on others was only the overflowing of their own pain.

Because all his thought was for others and none of his thought was left for himself, there was no thought that the devils could find to attach their torture to. When they reached to lay hold of him, they found nothing to lay hold of. No thought of self was there. He had given himself away.

How can you burn down a house when the owner of the house has himself set it afire so that you may warm your hands against the cold?

How can you cast a man into the sea when he himself has already leaped in to save you from drowning?

Then the devils howled with fear and rage. For the devils saw that the eyes of love see clear through Hell. When a devil is loved, how shall he keep on being a devil? When Hell becomes an Abode of Love, is that not very much the same as Heaven?

XIII

THE PRAYER OF PRAISE

❧ *Delighting in delightfulness* ☙

I said to the Master,

"What has praise to do with prayer? If God is not a person, why should we praise Him?"

The Master said,

"We do not praise God for His sake, but for our own sake."

I have a feeling that if only we had the power of hearing keyed to such a pitch, we should hear the sun and all the stars singing praises. What a hallelujah that must be, where the heavens are His choir stalls and the starry singers march like thunder glittering through the voids of space!

But they do not sing out of God's lack; they sing out of their excess.

So it is meant for us.

God is not a person. God is not a hungry tyrant listening for the flattery of men and angels.

God does not need our praise of Him. We need our praise of Him.

The prayer of praise is a mighty prayer. It is our blessing on the world and on ourselves; for it is a song of joy, as flowers are a song of joy and light is a song of joy; and it has the power to fill emptiness like flowers, and darkness like light.

A prayer of praise is man's spirit putting on the armor of cheerfulness.

A prayer of praise is our mind's taking delight in the delightfulness of all delightful things—and adding to the sum of this delightfulness.

ᴥᴔ When we praise God ᴖᴤ

When we praise God, all our thoughts rise up and dance at the top of the hill of the mind. All the cells of our body sing. Our blood runs like a singing stream in our veins and our bones wax joyous.

All there is responds to a word of praise. God responds. We respond. Everything responds. The whole world sparkles, quivers, comes alive. Things vibrate and are quickened. We vibrate and are quickened. Heaven and earth are in tune with us, and we are in tune with them. When we give praise, everything wants to give in return. Everything wants to do things for us.

It is almost as if when I say, "What a beautiful world!" the world tries to be beautiful; it glows and puts on its loveliest airs. And when I say, "Thank you, God!" God pours forth His gifts to meet my thankfulness.

ᴥᴔ Ah, little piccolo ᴖᴤ

Listen.

God is conducting His symphony. All the horns and drums of heaven roll forth His joy in the world that He has made.

When you sound your prayer of praise, God smiles and whispers, "Ah, little piccolo! I was waiting for you!" Then he lifts His hand and all His horns and drums echo like a grand reprise your joyous note.

Your life is not a little one-note nothing, dreary, weary, out of tune, but part of the living song of life.

Listen. The world is a song of joy. God is singing—dancing, too, no doubt. This world is the song He sings.

Sometimes our ear catches dissonances, sometimes even silences. But a harmony embraces dissonances, and a song sings even through its rests.

Life is the song of the spirit of joy rejoicing in its own joyousness, joyous even through its pain.

For the joy of God is beyond laughter—or tears—as life is more than these. And we are lifted to the highest peaks of joy, not so much through smiles and laughter, but by noble thoughts and greatness of heart and steadfast action.

❧ *Only what is possible* ❧

All prayer should end with praising God.

Prayer should begin with praise, too. But sometimes when we set out to pray, try as we will, we have no heart for praising.

We are fortunate to be able to find the strength to pray, let alone praise.

So if sometimes we start out to pray with a heavy heart, let us pray heavy-hearted.

God knows our heart. God knows its capacities and limitations. God knows what we can and what we cannot do.

God only asks what is possible of us; He lets us ask the impossibles of Him.

God pushes us beyond ourselves—but only when He knows, though we do not, that we are capable of going farther.

God stretches us—but to the growing, not the breaking point.

Start your prayers with praise—if you can.

But pray whether you can praise or not.

Pray until you can praise. Let this be your rule.

❧ *To rise high enough* ❧

To pray with praise affirms your faith.

It is a way of saying,

"God, I believe.

"I may not see the good. But I know the good is there.

"The good has to be there. Because you are there. And you are good."

In our human world nothing is complete. We see only beginnings and endings.

Our life is like listening to music a note at a time, or reading a book a word at a time.

To praise God is to hail the wholeness of things!

Now we see darkness. To praise God is to glorify the light that has no shadow cast by turning.

To praise God is to affirm life where we see no life and strength where we see no strength.

To praise God is to expect supply where we feel need and joy where we feel sorrow.

To praise God is to be at peace in the midst of conflict and to find love at the center of disorder.

To praise God is to affirm the light that is beyond light and darkness. It is to affirm the love that is beyond love and hate. It is to affirm the life that is beyond life and death. It is to affirm the joy that is beyond joy and sorrow.

To praise God is to enter into the place of stillness in the eye of the whirlwind, and into the calm that is deeper than the waves of the sea.

To praise God is to rise beyond the clouds and come out upon the shining.

Make no mistake. The shining is there. You have only to rise high enough. To praise God is to rise high enough.

⋘ By trying to be like Him ⋙

How do we make a prayer of praise? Shall we cry out, "Praise Him!" or exclaim, "Thank You, Lord!"

"Glory, glory, glory!"—is this the shout we should raise?

Words are a way of praising. Words are good. We human beings are word-people. We need words. We communicate, find release, and express ourselves through them.

But we can praise God in more ways than by words.

We can praise God by rejoicing in His works and in His world. God is good; the world He made is good; we are good. We praise Him when we live as if this were so.

Above all, we praise Him by trying to be like Him.

Is there any higher praise than this?

To seek to be like God does not mean to seek vainglory. It does not mean that we puff ourselves up and pretend that we are gods.

We are most like God when we call forth those qualities in ourselves that are godlike.

You are the human child of God. Seek to rise to the divinity that is the highest element of your humanity.

The highest name men have for God is love.

So to seek to be like God is to seek to be like love.

If you seek God and find power, to praise God is to use that power, not so that people will say of you, "Wonderful!" but so that people will say, "Wonderful!" of the world you make with your power.

Love makes itself less than the least and places itself underneath everything else so that it can lift up anything that needs lifting up. Love supports everything. Love embraces everything. Love gives itself without holding back and without looking for gifts in return. Love loves without seeking—even for love.

To love is to praise God.

I cry out to God, "I am grateful!"

I am not everything; I am not even all I should be. But I am something. I shall not weep because I am not more. The god-spark is in me and I shed such light as I am able. I fall short, but I grow. And I give thanks that I am as much as I am and that I have been used by life to the extent that life has used me.

⤷ The reed the shepherd plucks ⤶

Sing praises. Shout praises. Whisper praises.

Praise Him with your thoughts.

Praise Him with your silence.

Let your breathing in and your breathing out be a song of praise.

Praise Him when you walk.

Praise Him for food and drink.

Praise Him when you wake and when you fall asleep.

Praise Him for all you have been and for all you have not been.

Praise Him for what He has given you and for what He has not given you.

Praise Him for all that has been, is, and is to be.

Turn your life into a prayer of praise, which is a song of joy.

Then you will live in tune with His good.

His mind will think its thoughts through you.

His power will do its works through you.

His love will do its will through you.

You will be the reed the shepherd plucks from the edge of the stream that is time and the world. God will put you to His lips and blow a merry tune of life through you.

XIV

AS TO POSTURES

❧ The fire of God ❧

I said to the Master,

"How can it be that God answers many different kinds of prayer? For some plead and beg on their knees. Others perform strange rites. Others affirm. Others speak no word at all, but only sit in silence.

"Yet God comes to them all, speaks to them all, responds to them all."

The Master said, "It is with God as it is with fire."

Then I saw that when man was very young he rubbed two sticks together with a little tinder, and fire came from the rubbing of the sticks.

Later he made matches, and fire came when he struck a match.

Then he discovered electricity and fire came when he made electricity leap across a gap.

Now he has pierced the atom, and from the center of the stuff he and his world are made of, comes fire.

Fire sticks, matches, electric sparks, atomic power—fire responds to them all.

For fire abides, secret, smoldering, at the heart of all things and when conditions are right, it is drawn forth into visibility.

The fire that the fire sticks draw forth may be small, but a huge blaze may be kindled from it.

The blind faith in a whispered plea may have but little power, but if it is persevered in, it may change a world.

As man learns more about God and his relation to Him, he is able to draw forth the fire of God more surely and more quickly. That is all.

The atom is a better source of fire than the rubbing sticks. When the tinder is wet, the rubbing sticks may give no fire at all.

So man should seek after God to discern what He is like, where He dwells, what is His nature, how to approach Him, what are the conditions that cause His fire to flash forth with greatest force.

God is like fire.

He only waits for us to call on Him.

He loves to have us draw Him forth.

He would warm our heart.

He would light our mind.

He would carry it, soaring, dancing, singing, upward on the flame of His Spirit.

He would make us one with His All-Good.

The fire of God burns, whether we turn to it with rubbing sticks or an atomic pile.

The fire of God burns, whether we draw it forth or not.

The fire of God burns.

Even when we make no effort to draw it forth, even then it comes flashing up through us, to shake us, to wake us, like lightning, like dawn—ever-flowing, ever-glowing, ever-blessing— burning to be used for the good ends of life.

The fire of God is burning within you.

It will set fire to your life.

✺§ *You can change the cup* ⸱❧

Prayer, as I have said, is not to change God.

If God is, He is good.

Even if you have thought of Him as a king on a throne; even if you have knelt in fear; even if you have crawled to Him on your face—it makes no difference.

Your prayer did not change God. Not ever. Prayer changes only you.

If you came out of your prayer with a new feeling about yourself and God, yourself and your world, your world and God, then your prayer worked.

For your prayer changed you—your attitude, your thought, your feeling—about yourself, about God, about your world, about your life, about whatever it had to change.

Prayer changes only you.

But this is all it has to change.

For when you change, everything changes.

The world as God sees it—as it is in reality—is the perfect outworking of His divine decrees, of eternal law, of creative principle. It is radiant energy in harmonious and infinite extension.

How can I even think of it except to say that it is a shoreless sea of light! Except to say that it is the world God made! God made it, and having made it, looked at it and saw that it was good.

But the world as I see it—what is this? The world as I see it is— the world as I see it.

It changes when I change.

The world as I see it is not the world as you see it. Not exactly, though nearly.

It is very little like the world a bird sees.

It is even less like the world a tree sees, I think.

Sees, of course, is an insufficient word.

Experiences is a better word.

Your world is the world you sense is there with your senses.

It is the world you conceive is there with your mind.

It is the world you believe is there.

It is the world you feel is there.

The way you see the world depends on many things—your reasoning power; your imagination; your emotional bent; your senses, their sharpness and your delight in them or dislike for them; your beliefs, influenced to a very great extent by the community and culture you happened to be born into; your hopes and fears; your ability to identify yourself with other human beings.

All these determine how you see your world.

You can see in a moment that your world would be different if you happened to have been born an Eskimo, an Australian Bushman, a New Yorker, or a Russian in Moscow.

Try to think of anything in your world—say, a skyscraper, a book, a kangaroo, a thunderstorm, or any other thing—and think what it would be like to experience this from the viewpoint of any one of these persons.

Different, would it not be?

Just what any one of these things is in reality is hard to say—this, too, would depend on your viewpoint of reality.

But certainly your view of it determines what it is to you.

The Bible, for instance, might be something to build a fire with to a Bushman; a collection of superstitions to a Russian; the word of God to you.

Think the Bushman's thoughts, and you live in a different world.

Think the Russian's thoughts, and you live in a different world.

You cannot change a thought without changing yourself and your world.

Most thoughts change you very little, outwardly.

Sometimes a single thought not only changes a man a great deal, it changes the whole world of man.

A single flash of insight!

A single conviction!

A single hope!

The flash of insight one man had many thousands of years ago about kindling fire! Think what that did to history.

Or Mahomet's solitary experience with the angel Gabriel in a cave!

Or Einstein's realization that $e=mc^2$!

Or Copernicus' comprehension that the earth is round!

Or Jesus' understanding, "I and the Father are one!"

One thought is all you need to change a world! Just one thought! Many times men have changed the world with just one thought.

Ordinarily, however, change comes slowly as the result of a slow accumulation of thoughts that gradually bend the mind and the world in a new direction.

Insight—and change—come step by step, rather than all at once.

But the only purpose of prayer is to change you—to change your thought, to change your feeling, to change your way of looking at things, to change your attitudes, to change your beliefs—to change, in a big word, consciousness.

Prayer is not to change God.

You cannot turn God on and off.

God is always on.

God is always there.

God is only good.

You turn yourself on and off.

You avail yourself of the everywhere-present good to the extent that you are able to partake of it.

God is the never-failing wellspring of the living water of life.

But you are the one who must drink from the well.

What is the measure of the cup you carry to it?

You cannot change the well—you would not want to if you could—but you can change the cup.

The cup is your consciousness.

And you change the cup of consciousness through prayer.

As to the words of your prayer; the kind of God you believe God to be; the way you approach God—you have only one question to ask as to them all.

Do they help you to drink of the living water pouring from the wellspring of Almightiness—or do they hinder you when you try to quench your thirst?

You are meant to live.

You are meant to live abundantly.

Prayer is to change you so that you can.

✌ On my knees? ✊

Different people pray in different ways.

Some pray on their knees.

Some pray prostrate, stretched out on their faces.

Some pray, legs crossed in the lotus posture.

Some pray standing upright, with their hands outstretched to heaven.

Some pray crouched on a bed of nails.

Some pray reclining at their ease.

"Is there a posture," I said, "that above all other postures is the posture of prayer? Should I pray on my knees, as many do?"

The Master said, "Every posture your body assumes is a prayer."

Then I saw that the language of the body is very old. We were speaking it long before we learned the language of words.

All living creatures speak this language.

Even plants droop as drought cuts them off from their source of life, and spring up tall and straight, dancing in every leaf-tip, under a reviving rain.

It is not different with us.

We droop, and need no words to tell that we are suffering from a drought of spirit.

We dance tiptoe, and need no song to say that we are joyously alive.

We bow our heads.

We grimace.

We snarl.

We smile.

We frown.

We lift our hand outstretched.

We shake our clenched fist.

We extend our arms.

We fold our hands palm upward in our laps.

No one has to tell our friend or enemy what is in our secret thought.

No one has to tell us.

I have a cat, Blackie. For many years he has communicated perfectly to his world and me what he is thinking—and in all this time he has never spoken a word. A quiet dignified cat, he hardly ever even meows.

And none of us have to speak a word to him, for him to know what we are about!

Human visitor or animal, he reads our silence quickly!

We may pray on our knees.

We may pray cross-legged in the lotus posture.

We may pray prostrate.

We may pray dancing, as David did.

We may pray beating our chest.

We may pray clapping our hands.

We may pray making the motions various rites require us to make.

What is important is that our words do not make one prayer and our body another. For we pray with our body as well as our words.

⋖§ *Like the warmth of the sun* §⋗

We should assume this posture or that when we pray not because the posture changes God's attitude toward us, but because the posture changes our attitude toward God.

All postures are as one to the One.

It is only we who may consider one above the other.

It is only we who may feel that we cannot reach Him unless we assume this pose or that.

The One waits.

He reaches out.

You do not even have to reach out; you have scarcely to turn in your thought; and He rushes to give Himself to you.

He is like the warmth of the sun. The sun does not say that you must stand on a hilltop, arms outstretched to have its warmth.

The sun pours itself in a flood of warmth that reaches even into the dark ravines and secret recesses of the earth. The sun reaches even to the seed that is buried in the ground.

God's light is more pervasive than the sun's.

It falls on the man flinging himself down willing and receptive before Him. And it falls on the man whose prayer is still only a seed-thought buried deep under layers of indifference and selfishness.

All men—the holy man and the thief, the good man and the evil man—are naked before this light, for it shines not from the outside in, but from the inside out. How shall we shield our soul from the light that shines from within the soul?

⋖§ *To reach the switch* §⋗

The posture your body assumes changes you and expresses your secret thought, just as much as the words you speak change you and express your thought.

If you believe that God is mighty and you are powerless, if you feel that God wants you to submit—or if you feel you want to submit—you will pray on your knees. If you petition a king, it is wise to come on your knees. Or even on your face, prostrating yourself.

Likewise, if you believe that priests have special power, you will pay a priest to pray with you or for you.

If you believe that rites and sacrifices move the gods, you will want to have them performed.

On the other hand, if you believe that prayer is mainly an exercise in discipline—of the body or the mind or the emotions—you are likely not to believe that kneeling or rites will help you. You are likely not to turn to priests for help; to a teacher, perhaps, but not to a priest.

You may teach your body to sit in certain postures or move in certain motions, as you feel helpful. You may practice breath control. You may take exercises to control your thinking.

You do not even have to be a believer to pray.

Some of the world's great systems of prayer have not been based on a belief in God.

Yoga is such a system.

Zen is such a system.

The yogin and the Zen master may believe in God—they probably do—but the mastery of the system does not depend on their being believers.

They follow the disciplines, that is all.

If you believe that God is law, will you cry to the gate, "Open!" Or will you do those things you have to do in order to open the gate and to pass through it?

If you believe that God is law, not a person, then clearly it will do you no good to beg and entreat the truth or to pray on your knees.

The electric current turns on as quickly for those standing up as for those on their knees; it may even be easier to reach the switch.

If God is love, then love will lift us from our knees and draw us under its wing.

We do not go on our knees for God, but for ourselves.

God responds to those who are on their knees and to those who are not on their knees.

The universe obeys its law.

If kneeling or whipping ourselves or fasting helps us to fulfill what we consider are the conditions of reaching the supreme Power, then we should do it.

But it is not God who demands that we kneel or whip ourselves or fast. It is our own need of self-abasement.

We have only to look to see that. The universe fulfills the wishes of the proud as well as the wishes of the humble.

Humility is not a virtue because it helps to get prayers answered.

Humility is a virtue for its own sake only.

⊰ *The alphabet of prayer* ⊱

When you truly learn to pray, you will pray at all times and under all conditions. You will pray on your knees and you will pray running. You will pray in church and you will pray as you work. You will pray at your accustomed times of prayer, and you will pray when there is no time to pray at all.

You will pray doing breathing exercises and when you are out of breath and when you are gasping for breath.

You will practice postures when you pray and you will pray in every posture and no posture—lying and sitting and standing and walking and running and jumping.

You will pray repeating your prayer a fixed number of times, and not repeating at all, and repeating until you forget you are repeating it.

For you will learn that prayer is more than postures, more than forms.

These are merely the alphabet of prayer. After we learn the alphabet, we do not go on repeating it; but we form the letters into words and the words into sentences—and sometimes even into psalms of faith in God and love for God and joy in His living, loving presence.

XV

OF WORDS AND TIMES FOR PRAYER

ঌ§ *Morning and night* ৷ই

I said to the Master,
"Tell me about the times when I should pray."
The Master said,
"Tell me about the times when you should not pray."
There are many times to pray.
When you wake in the morning is such a time.
And just before you fall asleep at night.

Another good time to pray is when you wake at night. Many times I wake and lie alone with my thoughts in the dark. Instead of worrying, I think of God.

I have found such wakeful moments to be a good time to pray for others. There is always someone I know who needs help. I can think of him; place him lovingly in God's keeping; see him in my mind's eye blessed and at peace; hold him in my heart's love.

Lying quietly in the dark, I have nothing to distract me. It is one of the best possible times to pray—usually in a short time I fall asleep again.

Also, we should all say grace before a meal. No one has a right to eat without giving thanks. No life belongs to us. No life is ours to take. All life is the gift of life itself.

Before we eat we should thank Him who is the source of life and acknowledge that the life we take for our own use is not ours but His.

Saying grace before a meal helps us to see ourselves in right perspective—as part of the life-process.

Moslems are expected to pray five times a day—at dawn, at noon, at midafternoon, at sunset, and at dark fall. These are ritual prayers. The wording of the prayers, the manner in which they are to be made—these are fixed.

We need fixed times of prayer no less than Moslems do. When we merely memorize prayers and repeat them at fixed times, prayer may lose much of its power and importance; nevertheless, we need definite times for prayer and usually we need to have some method of prayer for these times that will be meaningful for us.

Everyone needs a few familiar words of prayer that have meaning and worth to him. Otherwise we are likely to be like the man who ran his car off a cliff. As it went over, all he could think of was, "God help the poor working girl!"

One time I ran over a small dog. I got out and picked him up. He was stunned and bleeding. As I carried him to his house, the only prayer that came to me was the line from a prayer learned in childhood. The Prayer of Faith, that Unity has taught to many persons—"God is your help in every need."

But I was grateful for that line. I kept my mind fixed on that.

Be still and know

I have had many different prayers that have meant much to me at different times in my life.

Perhaps the one I have liked most of all is the Bible verse: "Be still and know that I am God."

Just that. No more. I wonder how many scores of thousands of times I have repeated that simple sentence. I have said it aloud and silently. I have sung it—it has been set to music. I have said it slowly, one word on each breath; I have said it over and over as rapidly as I could think a sentence.

And how often I have felt—what? What words will tell you what God's presence is like? But fear and tension have subsided. Peace and love and self-control and health have surged up in me. I have been still and known that God is there.

Another prayer I have liked is this:

"I am a radiant, all-wise, all-loving, all-conquering son of God. I rule supreme in all the affairs of mind and body."

Sometimes I take one idea from the prayer, such as, "I am a

radiant son of God," and I try to keep this thought uppermost in my mind for a day. The next day I take another idea from the prayer.

Sometimes I sing a song-prayer. Usually I sing silently to my-self. Perhaps, if I am alone, I sing aloud.

Such a song-prayer is this:

> Oh, I am made whole!
> Oh, I am made whole!
> I am quickened and strengthened
> Mind, body, and soul.
> Through me now flows the life-stream,
> Free its cleansing waves roll—
> I enter the current
> And I am made whole.

Especially when I feel the need of prayer for healing am I likely to use such a song-prayer. I sing it over and over. I try to fill my mind with a sense of the wholeness of God. I try to feel myself being made whole. I try to sense the surge of healing in my body.

Another prayer I sometimes like is this:

"God is love. God, I relax in your healing love."

I say such a prayer-statement slowly, carefully, letting the weight of its meaning sink into my mind.

"God is love. Lovingly in the hands of Love, I place myself." This is yet another prayer-statement I have found meaningful.

A prayer I have often used as I go to keep an appointment or meet a situation that seems challenging is this: "I go to meet my good."

When I have dealings with others, as I have said, I often use the prayer, "I behold the Christ in you." This is a statement I especially use when I find myself having disagreeable thoughts about the person I am dealing with. As such thoughts try to rise in my mind, I simply substitute the thought, "I behold the Christ in you," and usually I am soon able to.

Sometimes my prayer consists of single words. Thus I may pray, "God, you are my life." Or merely, "Life, Life, Life," repeating the one word over and over, seeking to wrap myself in the awareness of life, to feel it around me and through me, bathing me, sustaining me.

Or I may take other words, such as "Joy," "Health," "Supply," "Peace."

❧ *Divine order* ❧

A phrase I have used as a prayer countless times is simply, "Divine order." Sometimes I say, "I am in divine order." Sometimes, "Divine order is now established in me through the power of the indwelling Christ." But most of the time, I just say, "Divine order."

I know no prayer that seems to have more power. I use it when I am looking for a parking space, looking for a lost object, trying to get a balky machine to work, blessing an inharmonious situation, blessing an irate person—possibly me—and in innumerable other instances.

There is no question that I use these words, "Divine order," as a kind of magic, a charm, a spell.

But there is also no question that the words have a kind of magic. They work.

I have seen lawnmowers start, machine parts slide into place, taxicabs appear in improbable places, rain fall.

Sometimes to my own wide-eyed astonishment.

Sometimes when I have used this simple prayer, "Divine order," I have felt like the cleric who came on a young man cursing and kicking a tire that would not come off a wheel. The cleric admonished the young man to pray instead of curse. The young man agreed, and the two prayed. As they did, the tire slipped quietly off the wheel and the preacher involuntarily let out an oath.

I have seen such unbelievable results from this single prayer that I have wondered what can be happening.

I have decided that the prayer, for one thing, does something to me; it helps me to get myself in divine order.

And when I am in divine order, certainly I am in touch with unbelievable power.

For order is the rule of the universe; when we put ourselves in order, we align ourselves with the power that moves through the world. Then the power of life flows unobstructed through us and through all that is around us.

We move with the movement of the universe, and everything falls into its right place.

In an ancient story, Thor, the Thunder God, in one of his innumerable contests with the giants, is challenged to drain a simple-looking drinking horn. Much to his chagrin, he cannot. Later he discovers that the innocent-looking goblet is magically affixed to the oceans, and when he lifts it to his lips—quaff as he will—he cannot drain it. All the waters of the world are keeping it full.

Divine order.

What a simple phrase, as simple as Thor's drinking horn.

But the whole universe is framed around it, pours through it, and is expressed by it.

When we utter these simple words, we lay hold of that which is the foundation of the earth and holds the stars in their places.

We are uttering the prayer of attunement; we are walking in the way; we are making our will one with the one will. Then infinity itself is working through us.*

৺ঌ To pray aloud ঌ৺

When I can, I like to pray aloud.

I have found that silent thought does not have the power to control my mind that speaking aloud does. This is especially true if I am in a troubled or anxious state.

When I speak a word aloud, it commands the attention of my mind. Speaking a word aloud helps me to do what I am seeking to do in all my praying. It focuses my thought and instead of leaving it turning on itself moves it where I want it to go—toward God.

This is the real end and aim of prayer—to turn our thought off ourselves, off our trouble, off our pain, and direct it toward God.

When we have found a way of prayer that does this—whether it be repeating Our Fathers or Nembutsus, or merely disciplining

* For more affirmative prayers to use in various situations you may find yourself in, see page 257.

our thinking—let us hew to it with all our mind and heart and strength, for we have found a way of prayer that is life itself.

◦§ To my green edge of growing §◦

Words have no power in themselves.

I say words only so that they will lay hold of my thought and direct it Godward.

As for me, prayer works when it takes my thought off myself and my troubles and places it on God.

To achieve this, I will sometimes repeat a prayer as rapidly as I can, giving my mind no time to slip to something else.

Or I will say it as slowly as I can, one word on each breath, bringing all my power of mind to bear on each word as I think it, breathing slowly in, breathing slowly out, quietly, rhythmically, all my energies relaxed but fixed in focus on a single thought.

Have you ever thought how a tree grows? Out at the end of the trunk, out at the end of the branch, out at the end of the twig, out at the end of the leaf—there all the forces of the life of the tree are focused and there the growth takes place.

Prayer stretches me out to my green edge of growing.

I want, then, a prayer that I can pour all my thought into, all my feeling into—prayer that will make such demands on me that I have nothing left over to give to anything but prayer.

I want a prayer that lays hold of me—body, mind, and soul— and points me utterly toward God.

If I use one prayer too long, I find that after a time it loses its power to keep me God-pointed. I repeat the words, but they have no power over my thought.

This is ritual praying, and the past tense of rite is rote. When a prayer becomes rote, it is meaningless.

For a prayer is valuable only insofar as it seizes and holds our mind in the direction of God and His good.

◦§ To a razor edge §◦

Many people like to use Bible verses as prayers.

Unity puts out a little magazine of daily meditations, *Daily*

Word. My wife keeps the magazine on the window sill above our kitchen sink and the first thing in the morning as I drink a glass of water, I read the lesson for the day and meditate on the affirmative prayer that is always at the top of the page.

Often I use this prayer throughout that day.

We all need a few favorite prayers that we use at regular times. After a while we may want to change these, but we may come back to them.

I use simple prayer statements, usually short ones, and I repeat them over and over.

I seek to concentrate all my thought on them, to sink my mind in them.

I am not one who can long repeat Hail Marys and Our Fathers. I could not spend my life saying over and over as many Buddhists do, "Namo Omito Fo." Prayer wheels humming, *Om Mani Padme Hum*, would have little value for me.

This does not mean that such practices have no value.

I can see their value for some. They have a gyroscopic value. They automatically stabilize the thought of the person who uses them. In a crisis, he repeats the sacred words almost without thought. This is their value.

He goes forward, as it were, against the foe, murmuring *La ilaha illa Allah*, even if he is so frightened or troubled that he cannot think. Part of his mind remains God-pointed.

There is no question that this is much better than merely giving way to terror, confusion, and disorder, as many do.

But above all to me, prayer is a focusing of my mental powers, a marshaling of my spiritual forces.

Prayer makes man whole because it brings the whole man to a God-point.

Prayer, at its highest, grinds my thinking, whets my soul, hones me to a razor edge of Spirit.

❧ Is an apple? ☙

The great purpose of prayer is this—to turn longings into words; to turn words into attitudes; to turn attitudes into acts; to turn acts into a life.

Prayer does not end in words; prayer begins with words.

All too often praying people get lost in the words of their prayers. The words become the end-in-itself. But the words are not the end-in-itself.

The word God is not God. The word love is not love. The word peace is not peace. The word life is not life.

We are not alive just because we say, "Life! Life!"

We do not become aware of God just because we speak His name.

We do not love others just because we say, "I love you."

We are not at peace because we cry, "Peace, peace!"

We may repeat a prayer over and over until we ourselves get to thinking that merely because we have so often repeated the name of something we want, we have the thing itself.

Too often we mouth words as if they were facts.

But a thing and the word that stands for it are not the same thing.

We can say, "Apple! Apple!" till we are starved but we shall not have an apple till we take one in our hands—shiny, red, round, and smooth, crunch the pulpy fruit between our teeth, and feel the sweet juice spurt through our lips and against our tongue. Then we have an apple even if we do not know the name for it.

We are not likely to make this mistake with an apple and confuse the fruit with the word for it. But with God or peace or order or love, this is an easy mistake to make.

Many people think of themselves as religious because they keep their minds frothing with religious words and phrases although they live selfish, empty, loveless lives. Words are not enough.

Not that words are bad. Words are not bad. Words are good.

They are what prayer begins with.

⊰ *Prayer begins with words* ⊱

Words are what prayer begins with.

Better to think about God and to cry out His name than never to think of Him at all. Better to think of love and to keep one's mind turned to it than never to think of love at all.

Even when our prayers are merely words, they have value.

We are like the boy who was taught to repeat a secret word. He did not know the meaning of the word, but he said it over and over. He wandered over the earth, having many adventures. Everywhere he never failed to repeat the word, because he believed it had power. One day while he was saying it, a strange man touched him on the shoulder, and said, "I hear you speaking my name. I am the lord of this country. What is it that you want with me?"

Our prayers begin with words. And words have power.

If you cry out the name, "God," long enough and often enough, even if you do not know what it means, one day God may answer and cry out your name. After that, your life will not be the same again.

If you cry out the word, "Love," and think about it often enough and affirm that you are loving and that you are loved, sooner or later the essential meaning of the word will seep down through your mind as water seeps down through the cracks of a rock, and you will find yourself having to give yourself in love, whether you want to or not.

There are Buddhists who cry after the name of God all their waking hours every day of this life. "All hail our God! All hail our God!" They repeat the cry over and over, grind it out as if upon a grindstone.

But the word is a grindstone. The word grinds down the flint of their heart; the word hones the dull edge of their mind; and after a time a feeling that is more than a word cuts its way through into their life.

This can happen to the devout in all religions.

For words are power. There is a germ of power in every word you speak.

So there is value just in speaking the word, whether at first it means much to you or not.

ᴇᱫ Words, attitudes, acts, life ᱬᴇ

Words are like seeds. If you sow enough of them, even in barren ground, even among rocks, even among weeds, sooner or later one will sprout and grow.

Our prayers begin with words. And words have power. But they have greater power when we realize that they are not the end and answer of prayer. They are only the beginning.

They are meant to lead us into attitudes and acts and life.

For do we not think about God and call out for God in the hope that we shall come to feel that a divinity is with us? When we feel God's presence with us; when we feel that we have access to that which is more than ourselves; when we suddenly sense that there is that with us which is a help in our need—how much more than a word we have, then! When we feel a flash of unexpected power stir in us and in our affairs; when we feel a flash of unforethought—of wisdom in our mind; when we are suddenly quickened by a new idea or insight—this is to pray aright.

We see that we are not little and weak and powerless; we dare to act as if we had access to power and wisdom and love beyond our own; and we see things being moved and changed and altered in unexpected but good ways.

When we not only say that God is our help in every need, but really feel that God is our help in every need—with what courage and faith and joy we venture forward then.

Words are good, but they are only the beginning.

When we pray using words, we are as fishermen who fish with minnows. But we do not fish for minnows.

Words are the minnows we cast into the stream of mind and into the pool of being, hoping to draw forth fish.

This is the purpose of prayer—to take words and turn them into attitudes. To change not what we say about ourselves and life, but what we feel about ourselves and life.

We would not chew the word "apple" as if it were an apple; let us not chew the word "God" as if it were God or the word "love" as if it were love.

Prayer should be more than words. It should change our thinking. It should change what we feel.

When we have prayed, not only should we have spoken words of love, we should be more loving. Not only should we have spoken words of faith, we should be more faithful.

It is our attitude, not our words, that is important. It is what we do, not what we say, that changes life. It is better to be a professed atheist and to live a life of selfless service to our fellow men than to spend our days mouthing prayers to our God but serving only our own self-interest, even if we call our self-interest spiritual growth.

The great purpose of prayer is this—

To turn wordless longings into words of faith.

To turn words of faith into life-supporting attitudes.

To turn life-supporting attitudes into brave, wise, loving acts.

To turn brave, wise, loving acts into a full life.

XVI

THE ROLE OF THOUGHT

❧ *One single thought* ☙

I said to the Master,
"Is there a thought that is more important than any other thought?"
The Master said,
"What thought are you thinking now?"
Then I saw that we live thought by thought, feeling by feeling, word by word, act by act.
We live moment by moment.
What is your life of this moment?
Sometimes we think of life as something vast and fixed, stretching before us and behind us.
But we encounter life only a moment at a time.
And we can change it only a moment at a time.
And this is the only way we have to change it.
The thoughts I have thought are gone. Yes, even the thought I just had. I do not have to change them. I cannot change them.
The thoughts I will think are yet to come. Yes, even my next thought after this. I do not have to change them. I cannot change them.
There is only one thought I have power to change—the thought I am thinking this moment.
There is only one word I have power to utter or not to utter—the word I am speaking this moment.
There is only one act I have power to do or not to do—this moment's act.
I do not have to control all life.
I do not have to control all thought.
I do not have to control all acts.

I have only to control one single thought—the one I am thinking now.

One moment's life—this is all I have to control.

And even if I want to take on a larger task—this is all I can take on.

I encounter and live a moment's life at a time.

I think one single thought at a time.

Thoughts are like birds that fly by, like leaves that come falling through our grove of mind. We can see them as they go by, but we cannot catch them and hold them.

Thoughts are like bubbles that we blow with our mind. Would you run after bubbles? No, blow yet another bubble more perfect than the last.

Thoughts are like the strides of a runner. Before we can take the next stride, we have to let the last one go. We can take only one at a time. And that is all we have to take to run the race.

If I can choose what my present thought will be, I am free. As free as freedom can be.

Nothing that comes to me can disturb me.

All that comes to me can bring only peace and joy.

This one thing is all life asks of me: that I control this thought.

If I do this, I control my life.

I control all the forces of life, and they all rush to do my bidding.

Life is a door that opens on the universe. But the universe, vast as it is, can only get in through the door a thought at a time.

This is the only way eternity can get in.

This is the only way infinity can get in.

Infinity is hard even to think about, let alone to lay hold of, but I have only to lay hold of it a thought at a time.

This is the only way I can lay hold of it.

Think of that a moment.

I can lay hold of all that is, but only a thought at a time. And that is the only way all that is can lay hold of me.

Are you in charge of the thought you are this moment thinking? This one thought! That is all life ever asks of you.

If you can handle one thought, you have charge of your mind. You have charge of your life.

For life can only come to you a thought at a time.

If you can stand at the door and say to this present thought, "Enter in," or "Do not enter in," you are in charge of your life.

All the torments of hell—if such there be—can only come to you a thought at a time. All the temptations of earth can only come to you a thought at a time.

All challenges, all problems, all troubles, all hardships—they can only come to you a thought at a time.

Do you struggle with cosmic problems? Do they seem too vast even to comprehend? They are not too vast to comprehend—a thought at a time. And that is the only way they can be comprehended—or solved. A thought at a time.

You may not feel that you can handle all there is to handle, but you can handle all you have to handle—the thought you are thinking now.

Set down this book a moment.

Think of the thought you are thinking now.

In all life, you have no more important business than learning to control this one single thought.

Will life bring you pain and anxiety?

Will life bring you peace and joy?

What thought are you thinking now?

Are you in charge of this one single thought?

When you are, you are in charge of life and can yourself determine what life will bring.

✑ A *diamond mine* ঙ

I said to the Master,

"Is this then all there is to prayer? Controlling my thought?"

The Master said,

"There was once a man who owned a parcel of land. It was four-square and perfect in every way. But it was like all other land. The winds blew on it. The rain fell on it. In winter it was occasionally covered with snow. It was cloudy in season and sunny in season; once in a while it was too hot and dry; once in a while it was too cold and wet.

"But one day while he was digging in his land, the man discovered a diamond mine. Since he now had unlimited funds, he determined that he would make his land impervious to the elements, and this he set out to do. Slowly he wove a web of crystal over and around it, so that no rain could fall on it. When the sun did not shine, artificial lights made the crystal dome glitter as if it were the daylit heavens. When the sun shone too hot, shutters closed in the dome so that only the acceptable amount of light entered.

"The rain that fell on the dome was drained into reservoirs and thence was fed into the land in only desired amounts, too.

"So the man dwelt happily under his pleasure dome in a land that was never too cloudy or too sunny, too hot or too cold, too wet or too dry.

"In this perfectly regulated land, the man dug his diamonds and lived content while the earth kept spinning through space, carrying the man, his land, his diamond mine, and his pleasure dome, neatly, securely, and in perfect order—until one day the earth shook itself.

"The earth shook itself so lightly that the quake passed unnoticed except by the scientists who watch the seismographs on which all earthquakes are recorded. It just shook things up a bit. Just enough to give the man a moment's fright and rattle the cups in the cupboard. Then everything settled down again, and the earth went on spinning in space, carrying the man, his land, his diamond mine, and his pleasure dome.

"But down at the bottom of the mine, which was quite deep, a few days after the unnoticed earthquake, a little crack appeared. The crack widened and became a dampness, oozing up between the diamonds, from the unseen, unknown depths, whence the diamonds, too, must long ago have come. Slowly the dampness became a wetness. The wetness spread and became a pool. The pool bubbled up and became a lake. And the lake began to belch and smoke and send forth sulfurous vapors that in a short time filled the mine and turned the land into a stinking swamp. The air, smoky, sulfurous, and foul, filled the beautiful crystal dome that now served not to keep out the changing seasons, but to keep in the noisome atmosphere seething up from the unseen depths."

Then I said, "Master, if this is not the way, where is the way?"

The Master said, "There was a man who owned a piece of land.

The land was four-square, fertile, and pleasant. But it was like all other lands. Wind and rain and snow came there on occasion. It was cloudy and sunny and hot and dry and cold and wet.

"But the man built a house on the land. He planted crops—corn and potatoes and turnips and beets, and even a few petunias to please his wife. He bought a calf and raised it till it was a cow that gave him milk and calves. He planted trees, apple trees for fruit and oak trees for shade.

"One day, while he was digging his land, this man, too, discovered diamonds. But this man did not turn his land into a diamond mine. Instead, he continued to cultivate his crops, and searched for diamonds only when he had need. Then he would sell them in the market, where they brought a high price, for he loved the diamonds and even learned the art of diamond cutting so that he could make them shine with great luster.

"When the sun shone, he enjoyed the sun, for he knew that it made the crops grow. When the rain fell, he enjoyed the rain. He knew that it too made the farm a green and growing place.

"Sometimes he even walked in the rain. He liked the feel of the pelting drops against his face and hands. He built cisterns and ponds and when there was too much rain he caught and held it back so that when there was too much sun he could let the water trickle out to his thirsting acres.

"Before the winter set in, he chopped down some of his trees, so that when the snows came, he could sit, warm and happy, in front of the roaring fire he built in his house. There he sat on winter evenings, reading and resting and sometimes polishing his diamonds.

"One day an earthquake shook the land and the house and the man. It rattled the teacups and loosened a few stones in the chimney, but it did no permanent damage.

"Yet sure enough, in the corner of the land a crack appeared. The crack widened and became a dampness. The dampness spread into a wetness. The wetness became a bubbling pool. But the land had not been honeycombed to make it into a diamond mine, so the bubbling issue from the deep did not turn the whole area into a sulfurous swamp, and the vapors, not being enclosed by a crystal dome, dissipated quickly into the open air and were borne away by the wind.

"Indeed, the owner, tasting the waters, discovered that they had great cathartic value, so he enclosed the bubbling flux of vapors in a building to which he could repair on a cold evening for a warm medicinal relaxation in the waters of his own private spa.

"He even bottled these for his own use when he needed them and sold the rest to the sick. The vapors he piped into his house to heat it.

"So there he lived, happy and secure, cultivating his land, tilling his corn and potatoes, caring for his trees, tending his cattle, polishing his diamonds, bathing in his hot spring—and enjoying an ever-more-abundant life."

❧ All-mite and Almighty ❧

Then I felt confused.

I said to the Master,

"A moment ago you told me that I should work to control my thought and now you tell me it is not enough to control my thought. What then shall I do?"

The Master said,

"You must do everything you can to take charge of your thought and you must do everything you can to put God in charge of your thought.

"They are not two things but one. They are the opposites that are the same.

"Only when you turn over your mind to God and let Him think His thoughts through you will you be able to control your thinking; and only when you control your thinking, will you be able to turn over your mind to God's direction so that you can think His thoughts."

Then I saw that it is like growing a garden.

To bring the garden to the harvest, I must plant the seed; I must water and till and weed and prune. The garden will not grow unless I work it. If I let the bindweed spring up between the green rows; if I let the cutworms ravage the young shoots; if I let the drought dry up the tender leaves—I will have little that is good to eat on my table.

Yet I do not grow the garden—the garden grows. The garden

grows not out of my work, but out of the seed and the earth and the sun and the rain, each living thing in the garden out of its own nature.

If I try to force the beans to grow as if they were corn, and the corn to grow as if it were watermelons, nothing will grow.

I must work as hard as I can and at the same time let everything be.

This is, also, what I have to do with myself.

I do nothing, but I do all. Only when I give my all-mite, does the Almighty give its almightiness.

I have to will to do what I can.

I have to work to do what I can.

But I have to be willing to let the will of God do its work through me.

Then I saw that the only man who is free is the man who has mastered himself, and only the man who is free can master himself.

You must gain control of your thoughts in order for your thoughts to be free, and only when your thoughts are free can you have them under your control.

When you search for God with all your heart, God will reveal Himself to you.

And when God reveals Himself to you, you will search for Him with all your heart.

To become master of the instrument, I must submit to its disciplines.

In order to hit the mark without taking aim, how many weary times must I throw the awkward dart!

In order to play the piano without taking thought, how many weary years must I practice my scales!

It is water power that turns the wheel, but I must set it in the stream; and for what shall I set it in the stream except to have the water turn it!

I am only the match. I am not the fire. But to ignite the fire, I must set fire to myself.

I work as hard as I can work so that God may do His perfect work through me.

I pray God to work through me so that I may do my perfect work.

Seven-league boots

To pray is to reach.

We try to be the best we can be. We strive to do the most we are able to do.

Yet everyone knows in some part of his nature that it is possible to be better than his best, and possible to do more than he feels able to do.

We have to do everything we ourself can.

We have to strain to our own utmost.

Then we have to let go.

Then we have to let God.

To pray is to reach beyond ourself.

To pray is to reach for what we cannot ourself lay hold of.

We stretch. We stretch to the utmost.

We devise.

We practice every stratagem we can.

Then God lays it in our hand.

I wonder if great achievement—true creative accomplishment—ever comes in any other way.

Creative work is always a free gift—but it is given only to him who earns it.

"The idea came to me," we say.

I wonder if anyone ever thinks of an idea in any other terms.

It comes floating silently out of the nowhere and neverwhen within you.

You think and think, and then suddenly, without effort, appearing almost like an apparition, silent, subtle, whole, from nowhere at all, there the idea is.

Hardly ever are the thoughts we consciously think good enough.

They march along, lockstep, goosestep—one, two, three, four—and they get from here to there.

But this conscious kind of thinking never takes us outside ourself. These lockstep thoughts never rise as thought can do—suddenly, magically—and transport us out of the barracks and the prisonhouse of self. They never whirl us to the top of life for a shimmering, soaring, unexpected, exciting vision of truth.

Prayer is thinking—but prayer puts seven-league boots on our thinking.

We may still have to go forward step by step, but prayer takes us seven leagues at a step.

Suddenly there we are when we pray—at a point beyond our own power to go.

We can take a step seven leagues long or high or deep.

We can step to a peak or a deep of thought. We could never get there by ordinary means. But prayer carries us there at a single bound.

✂ Two kinds of thinking ✃

There are two kinds of thinking—and we have to do both. But too many of us accept the first kind and never—or hardly ever—look for the second.

The first kind of thinking is planned. We outline where we are going and we go there by the route we have outlined.

"I am going to the bank and deposit my check," we say. We know where the bank is. We know the streets that lead to it by the shortest route. We know when we have to go straight ahead and when we have to turn. And we follow the way we have planned.

But there is also a kind of thinking where we go for a hike in the woods. We start out across a field, go on into a grove, and come out of that upon a hill. We do not set out for any particular point. We set out to see what loveliness will happen our way.

Shall we cross the brook? Or shall we clamber along its bank? Shall we climb over the fence? Or shall we walk beside it till we come to the gate? We do not know until we get there.

And sometimes, as all you who hike in the woods are aware, sometimes we do not walk. Sometimes we soar. Yes, as if on wings!

Those of you whose thinking sometimes soars know that soaring is not premeditated; it is a kind of surprise gift, though not altogether unexpected either.

Suddenly there you are among the clouds!

I doubt if those whose thinking is always a planned march plan many excursions among the clouds. The clouds are hard to reach. Even those who have learned to soar cannot make soaring happen. They just put themselves in the frame of mind where it is likely to occur—and sometimes it does.

Then, there they are with a cloud-high view of things, an altogether new perspective, sometimes a little frightening, perhaps, dizzying, but nevertheless delightful. Sometimes, soaring, lost among the clouds of thought, they make a discovery no one has ever happened on before.

But, you may say, how often do I have time for a hike in the woods? I have banking to do.

Perhaps. But even on the way to the bank, you can turn left instead of right and follow a different route. Who knows what surprises life may bring you if you leave yourself free and invite surprise.

This I know, that lockstep thinking never produces more than lockstep results.

Only when you set your mind free will your mind take you somewhere you have never been before.

It is not easy to set the mind free.

One, two, three, four, down the well-worn road we trudge. The results are satisfactory. We get where we set out to go. We get from the known to the known.

We have learned how to walk. And walking is an adequate means of locomotion. To fly is very very hard—and we see no wings!

This, however, I know. They only find wings who have to fly.

The rest of us go plow-horse-plodding on.

Most of us accept the acceptable. We settle for the attainable. We pursue the possible.

We recall what happened to Icarus. There was one who was not content to walk. He strapped wings of wax upon his back and soared up toward the sun. The sun melted his waxen wings and he tumbled to his death.

I, too, recall what happened to Icarus, but what I remember about him is that he died flying.

It is not easy for us wingless ones to fly. It is far easier to walk along the ground. This we have learned to do, and we settle for it.

Perhaps, when we are little boys we try flying once or twice—we climb out on a porch roof with an umbrella or a stretched-out sheet and jolt down thump! upon the hard and bruising ground.

We feel lucky that we did not break a leg.

And so we give up.

This, too, I know—those who learn at last to fly are not those who give up.

We have to be willing to try our waxen wings again and again, to shape and reshape them, and even, alas, not to rise, but to thump down, bruised and shaken and humiliated again and again.

Flying is not easy—but is there anything that human beings greatly prize that is?

Do you want to fly? Enough to try and keep on trying? If you do, you can fly.

Of course, man flies every day now. Somewhere a plane is taking off this moment. Flying is now as familiar as walking.

My comparison has lost its savor, hasn't it?

But why?

Because someone was not content to walk.

Because someone dared to follow his bent up a path where no one before had gone—and at the top of this path he found wings.

There are no unattainables. There are only ends we have not yet attained.

There are no impossibles. There are only things we have accepted as beyond our power to do.

Often, to pray is to research for something impossible—and sometimes, to pray is to lay hold of it!

But whether we get what we pray about or not, we are trying our wings—and perhaps, we are finding them.

We are trying to be more than we have been.

We are refusing to settle for less than we might be.

We are stretching our mind toward God—and that is toward more truth and life and love and beauty and good.

Prayer is a venture into the unknown.

Prayer is a way of reaching beyond ourself.

Prayer is wings, O wingless one!

XVII

PRACTICE TO RELAX

✌ *Be still* ॐ

I said to the Master,

"Is there a way of prayer that will teach me to control my thought and to reach beyond thought; to master myself and to become more than self; to realize my own powers and to contact a higher power than I ordinarily have access to? There must be a way that is my way above all other ways. What steps will I take to get there?"

The Master said,

"Be still."

I was as still as I knew how to be.

The stillness reached into my body and my bones. My blood pulsed but slowly in my veins. Without effort, I remained unmoving, and the earth held me up. If my eyes looked, they did not see; if my ears listened, they did not hear.

Yet in my mind my thoughts ran to and fro. Like a bird fluttering and twittering from twig to twig among the dancing leaves, my thoughts fluttered and twittered from dream to dream in the tree of my mind.

This was the stillness of lying down and taking rest. I was as one who slept but dreamed.

Then the Master said, "Be still."

I was as still as I knew how to be.

The stillness spread from my body into my mind and into my thought, where the bird sang no more in the tree, but slept, for it was night.

For then I was as one who sleeps and does not dream or stir. My body was at rest. My mind was at rest.

Feeling ceased. Knowing ceased. Through the abyss of nothingness, I sank into oblivion.

This was the stillness of dreamless slumber.

Then the Master said, "Be still."

I was more still than I knew how to be.

The stillness reached through my body and my mind into myself. I passed out of the house of dreams and out of the cave of sleep into the soul of stillness. Here my heart did not beat, but I was myself the beating of a Heart. Here my mind did not think, but I was myself the thinking of a Mind. Here unfeeling ceased. Unknowing ceased.

I cannot tell you of this stillness save that it is no truer to say of it that it was soundless than to say that it was sound, for it spoke to me. It is no truer to say of it that it was dark than that it was light, for I saw. It is no truer to say that it was nothing than that it was something, for I was one with the One that is Many.

It was like seeing what sunlight is like, not by looking at the sun as it rises in the morning or sets in the evening or rages in the noonday sky—but from the center of the sun itself.

Then becoming ceased. There was only being.

My body was still.

My mind was still.

I was still.

This was the stillness of oneness with God.

⇜ *First you do nothing* ⇝

I said to the Master, "In praying, what do I do first?"

The Master said, "Before you can do anything, you must do nothing."

I thought about this.

I thought of the sea, the powerful sea, and saw how before the tide of the sea gathers and begins to pound at the cliffs, the tide ebbs and the waters draw away and the level of the sea sinks as low as it can sink. The more the tide recedes, the higher the tide returns.

I thought of the waves of the sea that can hurl ships as if they were straws and sometimes grind an island into sand and shingle. I saw how under the waves, where the wave begins, there is stillness and calm deep. If I could dive to the root of the wave, I could lie at my ease.

I thought of air. Next to the sea, I thought, the most powerful thing is air, for it is in the air that the wind rises and becomes storm. I saw that at the center of the storm, where the storm begins, there is quiet, there is no motion at all.

Out at the edge of the storm, the winds may knock down a forest or smash a city into rubble, but at the center, in the eye of the storm, a hummingbird can hover.

In the most powerful storm of all—in the tornado—at its center, where it begins, there is nothing. Nothing at all. A vacuum. It is because of this willingness first to be nothing, that the storm is able to become so powerful.

I thought of sea and wind. What are sea and wind but water and air?

If you were seeking a symbol of powerlessness, is anything better than water? When we want to speak of something as utterly acquiescent, we say, "It is like water."

So it is also with air. When we want to speak of something as utterly insubstantial, we say, "It is like air."

"An airy nothing!" we say.

But this airy nothing, willing to be blown anywhere, and this acquiescent water, willing to take the shape of any bowl—these are the two most powerful forces on the earth.

Then I wondered about fire. At the root of fire—where the fire begins—is there a dance of atoms, or is it still there, too? If I could go to the center of the sun, could pass through all its waves and winds of fire, there—at the center—would I find calm stillness and no heat at all? I wonder.

Nothing is more likely to get where it wants to go than a river. Not even mountains can stand in its way. Yet it gets where it would go without forcing; it merely seeks a lower level.

And a wheel—a wheel in order to turn must have a steady hub. The less movement there is at the center of the hub, the more power there is at the rim of the wheel.

Standing still is not being inactive. For the whole world moves from a central point of power. When you stand still, you let the power that moves the world move you. When the power that moves the world moves you, you travel, not down byroads and blind alleys, but along the main line of life.

Then I saw that to stand still is to take the first step in prayer.

❦ You learn to be still ❧

I thought how I might learn to be still.

It should not be hard, I thought, because it is natural. We were all still before we were active, and all our activity comes only out of stillness.

Yet I saw that many are never still. They whistle and talk and cry; they drum with their fingers and tap their feet and crack their knuckles. They fidget and scratch and blink. They bite their fingernails and pace back and forth. Even in their sleep they grind their teeth, snore, tremble, jerk, and twist.

Even in their prayers, some try to storm God. They pile words on words and acts on acts, and multiply rites.

This is not the way to Him. Although there is nothing between us and heaven but an attitude, we cannot force the gate.

Peace is a city we cannot take by might; until faith opens the gate and lets us through, we cannot enter.

To go beyond ourself, we must let ourself go.

Before we can let God, we must let go.

How do we let go?

There is a prayer that is a discipline and there is a discipline of prayer. You can master the discipline of prayer. To do this, you have to learn the art of letting go—how to relax.

To master a discipline demands practice. But do not make the practice hard. There are two reasons for not making it hard. One, you will not do it. Two, it defeats itself—a drill in relaxation should be relaxing.

In practicing relaxing, do what makes you most comfortable. It is probably best to lie down. If you cannot lie down, sit down. Choose a comfortable chair. A straight-backed chair is best for most of us; but choose a chair that makes it easy for you to relax.

Put your feet on the floor. Let your hands lie in your lap or hang by your side. To begin with, sit erect. Let the floor hold up your feet. Let the seat of the chair hold up your body. Let the back of the chair hold up your back. The floor and the chair are able to do this. You do not have to hold yourself up.

If you can, lie down. If you can be comfortable, stretch out on the floor; but your bed is all right. Do what makes it easiest for you. So stretch out comfortably, easily. Let your hands lie by your side. You can cross your legs or stretch them out; it may help to put a pillow under your knees. Also, it may help to take a pillow and with each hand holding a corner, pull it down under your head against your shoulders. Then your head will lie comfortably back in the cup that is formed in the pillow.

As I say, make yourself comfortable, whatever comfortable is to you now. If it means crossing your legs, cross them. If it means folding your arms, fold them. Start where you are. As you go on with the drill, as you relax more and more, as you become more aware of tension and want to let it go, you will not continue to maintain a position that is tense, because you will no longer feel comfortable in a tense position. You will untie your knots and let go every posture that requires energy for you to maintain it.

Watch a cat. A cat teaches us lessons in relaxing.

Watch a cat leap. First he relaxes, letting himself collapse into a ball of fur. Then he shoots up like an arrow!

Watch a cat relax. First he stretches, lips drawn back, ears pointed, limbs outstretched, toes extended, claws quivering! Then he tumbles in upon himself until he is a furry ball of nothingness. Prod him; whatever position you drape him in, there he hangs, effortlessly; he has let go, and no muscle is any longer contending against any other muscle.

The cat knows the ancient rule of the mystics, the Law of the Opposites. We can learn from his wisdom. To get tense, he relaxes; to relax, he gets tense.

So, stretch. Yes, make yourself tense. All over. Every muscle. Stretch. Yawn. Stretch. Yawn. Now let yourself go. All over. Every muscle. Just let go. As you stretched yourself out as far as you could, now let yourself fall in as far as you can. Just tumble in on yourself. In your thought. Your body will follow.

From tip to top

Stillness comes by stillness. The first step in stillness is to let go. Say to yourself, "I relax and let go."

If you cannot relax all of you—and you probably will not be able to—then relax part of you. Say to one hand, "I relax and let go."

Do not think of your hand as separate from you. But think of yourself as relaxing in your hand.

When you are relaxed in one hand, then relax in your other hand. Then in your arms, feeling tension going out of them from the shoulders down. Feel the tension running down from your shoulders, down through the nerves and muscles and veins of your arm, running down your skin as if it were water, and out of your fingertips—as if it were water.

When you have let all the tension run out of your arms and shoulders, then let the tension out of your feet and legs. Let your toes relax. Then your whole foot.

Feel what it is like to have no tension in your foot—to have your toes relaxed, and the ball of your foot, and across the arch, and in the heel, and up through the ankle.

Have you ever lain down in bed when you were very, very tired and had a great sigh of relief burst from your lungs? When you really relax your foot—just once—just such a sigh of relief will burst from your toes.

Relax one foot, then the other.

After you have relaxed your feet, relax your legs. Relax them from the hip down and let the tension run out of them as it ran out of your arms, like water.

I tell you to relax your arms and legs first because these are easiest for us to relax.

They are easiest to relax because we are more aware of them.

We do not so often issue direct commands to other parts of our body, so we are not so familiar with the feeling of tensing and untensing them.

We are used to telling our arms and hands and fingers and

our legs and feet to contract and to let go, to move and to lie still. So we know what it feels like to do both.

For this reason, it helps to start with them. We know when we have them relaxed. With the rest of our body we are not so sure.

We have probably consciously tensed and relaxed our abdominal muscles. So next we should practice with these. Tell your abdominal muscles to relax, and feel them let go.

Then try letting the muscles of your back and chest let go until you feel all the tension running out of them.

Hardest of all to relax is usually our face—because we are not aware that it is tense; we go around with it tense so much of the time. Our brow is wrinkled, our eyes are drawn into a squint, our jaw is set, or we are mumbling to ourself, usually unawares.

So here, too, we should relax little by little. Start with the forehead. Again start here because you have at times consciously tensed and untensed it. Feel it letting go, unwrinkling, smoothing out, relaxing.

Then move your thought to your eyes. As your forehead relaxes, you become aware of your eyes; and it becomes easier to relax the muscles that control them. Let your eyelids let go; let them fall shut and rest lightly together with no weight as they do when they are heavy with sleep. Now they are heavy not with sleep but with peace. Feel all the muscles that move the eyes about all day letting go. Your eyes hang heavy on their stalks, like sunflowers when the sun goes down. You no longer have any need to look at things. You feel your eyes sinking into your head. Your vision draws back deep within the shell of yourself as a turtle draws itself back into its shell.

Then let your jaw unhinge. Let it fall loose and free. Let go all rigidity. Let go all need to speak to anyone, especially to yourself. You have nothing more to say; you are past the need of words. You do not have to fasten your teeth in anything. Quit holding onto your tongue; let it sink to the bottom of your mouth. Feel what it is like to have the muscles of your tongue and jaw relaxed.

Then let go of the muscles that control your ears. Long ago we human beings gave up—except for small boys—the power to move our ears. But we still try. What are we listening for? The tiger lurking in the underbrush? This tiger is no longer there. You do not need to listen. You can let the valves of your ears close as you let them close when you fall asleep.

You can let all the muscles of your scalp relax. There is no reason for your hair to be standing on end; you have nothing to fear. Feel the tingling that spreads all over your scalp as the little muscles that control each hair let go their grip and let your hair lie down, lie smooth, lie soft.

From the tip of your toes to the top of your head you should be relaxed.

ৼ৽ The air comes out of the balloon ৶৹

Now you should be relaxed, all your muscles untensed. How are you breathing? Rapidly like a runner running a race? If you are, let this, too, let go. Take a deep breath. Then let your breathing relax. It usually helps to breathe deeply and slowly. But do not make breathing an effort. As you relax, your breathing will become deeper and slower. Now let it be natural and easy. As you feel the need of air, you let it into your lungs. When you are ready to let it go, you let it flow out again. Without taking thought, effortlessly. That is the way. Without thought. Slowly. Easily. In. Out.

As you relax, it may help you to think certain thoughts. Feel as if you were a balloon. Blow yourself up, up, up. Fuller, fuller, fuller. Then open the valve and let the air out. Imagine the valve in the top of your head, or in your big toe, or in your belly button, or wherever you want. Feel the air coming out, blowing away into its nothingness. Out of your head, out of your shoulders, out of your back, out of your arms and hands, out of your chest and abdomen, out of your legs and feet, emptying, emptying, emptying.

Have you ever watched a balloon as the air was running out of it? The balloon does not do anything; it just lets the air out; when there is no air holding it rigid, it just lets itself go.

It takes effort to blow yourself tense, as it takes effort to blow up a balloon. But to let go and relax, all you have to do is open the valve and let the tension escape.

Out—out of every muscle, out of every nerve, out of every vein, out of every organ, out of all tissues, even out of your bones, even out of your skin. You do not force it out. You just let it come out, let it blow out, let it blow away, let it be the nothing that it is.

❦ You learn to pray by praying ❧

In all this drilling, there are two things to keep in mind.

One. You are not a hand; you are not a foot. You are you.

You are not trying to relax your hand. You are relaxing you. You are not bits and pieces. You are a whole. You relax little by little, as you might untie knots in a string, one at a time. But it is the string with which we are concerned, not the knots. And it will help you as you relax in any part to keep in mind that this is not your hand and foot that is relaxing, but you.

Two. A drill in relaxing is not a necessary part of prayer. Thousands of human beings pray without learning to relax—and they pray effectively. A drill is a drill. Nothing more. But nothing less. It will help you.

People pray in many different ways. The way I am describing is one way; it is merely a way I have followed and a way many others have followed. People get help by following other ways than this. But also they get help by following this way. Thousands of persons have changed their thoughts, their lives, and themselves by following this way of prayer.

You learn to skate by skating and you learn to dance by dancing.

And you learn to pray by praying.

You may object that praying is not like skating and dancing.

Power in prayer, in meditation—you may say—is a creative power, a mental power, mostly a spiritual power. It is not a physical skill. However, we have a body, and we cannot divorce one part of us from what the rest of us is doing, and succeed. We cannot practice the postures of prayer while our mind carries us elsewhere. Nor can we think thoughts that are prayerful while what we are doing negates what we are thinking.

Certainly a creative skill like prayer takes more than mere repetition. Practice alone may not perfect you in it. But in the truest sense, I wonder if there is any skill that is altogether physical or mental or spiritual. Skating and dancing require creative genius —sometimes a great deal.

Mere repetition of a prayer will not produce an answer. Merely drilling in the silence will not produce silence.

Writing a million words may not produce a poem. Performing ten thousand experiments may not produce an electric light.

But it is true that most poets improve with practice. Occasionally a child almost without trying produces a poem. But most poets write a million words—or more—and throw them all away in order at last to produce poems.

A million words do not make a masterpiece, but they do make for improvement. So it is with prayer.

We all have an innate ability to pray—and to pray well—as we do to sing and to run. But the more we sing and the more we run, the better we become.

You can pray without practice—just as you can run without going into training.

But you pray better with practice as you run better with practice.

As a rule, the more we practice, the better we run.

And the more we practice, the better we pray.

At most things, we expect to have to practice.

We would laugh at anyone who felt he could play the piano without practice.

When a great musician tells us that if he does not practice for a single day, he knows it; if he does not practice for two days, the critics know it; if he does not practice for three days, everybody knows it—we accept this as true.

As any singer can tell you, we do not even know how to breathe well without practice—and a great part of learning to sing is learning to breathe well.

Shall we know how to pray without practice when we do not even know how to breathe without practice? Shall we be the master of our soul without practice when without practice we cannot even master a mouth organ?

⋖§ *They practiced* §⋗

The great masters of prayer—the saints and holy men of every religion—have been men who practiced prayer.

Jesus meditated for days, even weeks, at a time—at least once for forty days. Mahomet went again and again to meditate in his cave before the angel Gabriel appeared to him. Elijah went alone for forty days in the wilderness and then prayed alone in a cave before he heard the still small voice of his Lord. The Buddha spent seven years practicing the disciplines of his meditative way before enlightenment came to him.

And all these men taught their followers to pray—or meditate —regularly.

Certainly we can learn to relax by relaxing. If we never go beyond this physical skill—and it is only partly physical—we have learned a skill of infinite worth to us, and our whole life will be blessed by our having mastered it.

Almost everyone can improve his ability to relax. Most of us are tense when we do not know we are tense. When we think we have relaxed completely, we are still tense, unrelaxed in many parts of our body.

The ancients tell of the giant, Atlas, whom the gods tricked into taking the weight of the heavens onto his back to show how strong he was. Once he got it on his back, he could not let it go for fear it would collapse on top of him. So there he stands forever holding up the sky.

Like this giant, some of us carry the world around on our back and can never let go even for a second for fear that it will come crashing down upon us.

There we stand, as frightened as Chicken Little, every muscle taut, every nerve quivering, holding up the sky.

Instead of letting the earth hold us up, we walk around holding the earth up, holding ourselves up, trying to lift the world by the muscles of our mind. We have taken hold of our own soul's bootstraps—and we do not know how to let go.

∽§ A two-way street §∾

Practice relaxing.

But remember that just relaxing muscles is not enough. For many of us this is putting the cart before the horse. We are not tense because our muscles are unrelaxed. Our muscles are unrelaxed because we are tense.

There are none of us who will not profit by practicing relaxing. But we will profit more if—while we work at drills that help us to relax our muscles—we also follow a drill to help us relax mentally.

We are a two-way street. Every thought we take affects our body. Everything we do with our body affects our mind. We cannot change our physical condition without changing our mental condition. We cannot change our mental condition without changing our physical condition.

Probably we are not talking of two things but one—only we see the one from two different vantage points. When we look from one viewpoint, we say, Mind. When we look from the other, we say, Body.

So drills that teach us to relax our muscles help; drills that teach us to relax our thinking help.

We can improve our ability in both directions.

As we teach ourselves to change our thinking, we are like a person who goes to a hypnotist. At first the hypnotist may have to go through a considerable process involving many steps. He may have to explain what he is going to do and what the subject is going to do. He may even have to try different techniques. But once he has succeeded in hypnotizing the subject, each time he hypnotizes him again, it becomes easier. At last the hypnotist has only to say, "I will count to three, and when I say three you will be asleep"—or he has merely to snap his fingers.

In a sense, all of us move through life in a kind of super-hypnotic state. The master hypnotist has placed us in life's spell. He has suggested the limitations under which we have to operate; he tells us what we will see when we look; what we can and cannot do. From time to time he changes our limitations—

sometimes only for a moment—and we find ourselves with powers we did not know we had and with a creative vision almost beyond our comprehension.

The master hypnotist is ourself.

In Shakespeare's *Tempest*, there are two creatures. One is Caliban, a brutish lout. The other is Ariel, a winged sylph-like creature. They are both under the control of Prospero, the Master Magician—Ariel freely, Caliban reluctantly.

It is well to keep in mind that Caliban and Ariel are servants of Prospero.

We are not Caliban. We are not Ariel. We are Prospero.

We are not body. We are not mind. We are the Master.

Our mind-body is ours to direct and control, ours to master. The more we work to gain control of it, the better control we have. And the easier it becomes to get our mind-body to do what we want it to do.

Our mind-body is a great deal like a horse we have to ride—or sometimes more like a mule. It does what we have trained it to do—or what we have allowed it to do.

This beast we ride has its own inclinations. Unless we break it to our hand, unless we bring it under discipline, it may carry us where it will—and where we may not want to go. It may even try to throw us—especially if we have always given it its own head and followed its lead, and suddenly we try to force it in a new direction.

But if, slowly, patiently, daily, we have taught it to go forward and to halt at our command, to turn left at our "Haw!" and right at our "Gee!"—this brute beast will be docile and eager to obey us. It will trot and canter and gallop. It will take us, not down into the pastures and wallows that are its native haunts, but up the high trails of spirit where we would venture. It will leap walls at our command and hurl itself through rings of fire.

It may even be that we shall discover that the mount that has been given us to ride and master is not a halt and hobbled hack but a winged steed—even Pegasus. On his back, we may vault beyond the clouds, and even to the stars.

XVIII

A WAY TO TRANQUILITY

❧ *What is tranquil?* ❧

I said to the Master,

"When I have learned to relax my body, what more should I learn?"

The Master said, "It is good to know how to fall asleep when you would sleep. It is also good to know how to wake when you would be awake."

As you practice relaxing your muscles, you can also practice relaxing your mind. If you want to feel tranquil, practice thinking about tranquil things.

What is tranquil?

Waves breaking on a cliff—is this tranquility? Or a starry night? Or a wax-white water lily floating in a wax-black pond?

Tranquility is different to different people.

To the people of the East, the face of the Buddha is tranquility as perhaps nothing else is. Sometime, if you have occasion, look closely at a Buddha head; it may help you to understand what peace is.

Aloof, benign, serene, silent, the Buddha gazes at us through half-closed eyes and smiles a faint half-smile of triumph and composure, as tranquil as we are troubled, as perfect as we are imperfect. Beyond suffering because he sees through suffering to the cause, he looks through our swirl of circumstance to a reality untouched, untouchable by the wild swings of fortune's wheel that whirl the rest of us high or dash us in the mud.

Many of the great gods of Asia have such a look. To see to the essence of peace-in-action, look at a Siva Nataraja, a dancing Siva, if you ever have a chance. The god dances in a ring of fire; his matted hair streams from his head; his four arms gesticulate in four directions; his pounding legs batter the prostrate body of a dwarf; and all the time his face, expressively inexpressive, is motionlessly, emotionlessly fixed in an almost imperceptible smile.

In divine triumph and divine indifference, the Eternal whirls through its fiery dance of Time.

⋙ Spring, summer, and snow ⋘

Tranquility to many is a cigarette and a can of beer and a TV program pounding in their ear and jerking at their eye.

To millions throughout history tranquility has been a tranquilizer. From soma and haoma, the lost sacred drinks of the Hindus and Persians, through tobacco and alcohol, to LSD and sacred mushrooms, man has sought for peace in a potion.

Tranquility to some is a solitary walk in the woods. This it has often been to me. Peace is to walk alone on a spring morning when the birds are calling and the small shy wood flowers—violets and dutchman's breeches and trillium—have begun to bloom; with wild plum white at the wood's edge and deep among the larger trees the crab apple's rose-mist mounds.

Or go out on a summer afternoon and lie under a tree in the green shade, a few leaves dancing in the sometime breeze, a few clouds, large and white and lazy, drifting in the blue-bowl sky. Are these clouds that drift like thoughts, or are these thoughts that drift like clouds? After a while it becomes hard to tell whether the sky is in your mind or your mind is in the sky. It is like seeing a hillside mirrored in a lake. Sometimes you are not certain where the real hill is.

If it is winter, peace may be walking in the snow at night. Has it been a long time since you walked in the snow?

The snow comes down—cold, silent, white, not so much filling space as obliterating it. The familiar lines of every day slowly melt away. Nothing remains the same. After a while nothing remains.

Yet nothing is changed. The familiar world lies all around you. The same street, the same houses, the same trees. But for a moment you walk alone in an aloneness where emptiness has substance and formlessness finds form.

The snow's white perfection falls all around you—but try to lay hold of it and it melts on your fingertips and vanishes away. It is like the thoughts that fall across your mind when you are too tired for taking thought; you know that you think, but you do not know what you think.

This is nirvana, I feel sure, much more than night is or deep slumber. All things particular, definite, personal melt away. The snow, formless, insubstantial, universal, reduces you and the world to its common denominator—a white perfection; not nothingness, but making all things nothing; not intangible, but putting all things out of touch; not invisible, but making all things vanish.

Someone has said that when he wishes to relax, he imagines a waterfall in a wild and rocky chasm of the wood. The water rushes over the cliff's edge onto the rocks below in an uproar of mist and spray and waves, and thunders foaming through the gorge. But just beside the cataract a tree is growing. Among the slender twigs of the outmost wind-tossed branch of the tree a bird has built its nest. And there, above the dizzy precipice and churning water, the bird perches, singing.

This, he says, to him is peace.

ᕃᏟ A secret valley Ᏸᕽ

As for myself, I have a secret valley. If there is such a place on earth, I have never been there. But I go there often in my mind.

A river runs between high hills—almost like a fjord, I think, though I have never seen a fjord, and there is no precipitous rift of rock. The hills are high; I might better call them mountains. The river is broad, strong, and—I sense—deep, though I have never swum in it. I think it is a tidal river, a mighty tongue of the sea—and the sea, I know, is not far away, though I have never gone there.

But wide as the river is and high as the hills are, more impressive still is the dense green forest that descends in a green tide from the hilltops to the water's edge and rises green on the farther side to the green crest of the hills again, stretching green as far as I can see up and down the river from horizon to horizon.

I sense that the woods are full of flowers and birds and wild things, too. But my river is a river in a spell—silent, lovely, perfect—and I, too, am like one in a spell here. I do not walk—I am transported, swiftly, silently, along the river's length. From the road that runs atop the hills I always seem to have an almost unobstructed view.

Along this green river of revery, it is as if peace had fashioned a panorama, and I am part of it.

For many years I did not come here at will; I found myself here. I closed my eyes, and when they opened again, it was not on the world, but on an inner vision, this green world of my mind.

I never tired of coming here; so I practiced calling up this vision till I could come at will.

◁§ The meadow in the mind §▷

Perhaps none of these things—a dancing god, a spring morning, a summer hill, snowfall at night, a singing bird, a mystic valley— say peace to you.

I do not know what says peace to you. You will have to determine this yourself. But whatever it may be, bring it to mind. When you would relax and be still, let your mind dwell on some scene or experience that is your peace.

The Eastern mystics tell us that we should empty our mind. But this is like telling us that we should breathe out and not breathe in again. Most of us cannot empty our mind. Let us fill it, then. Let us fill it with whatever will help us to relax, whatever says peace to us.

Out of your life, there are a few scenes or experiences that are linked in your thought with tranquility. Perhaps it is something you remember. Perhaps it is something you imagine. This does not matter. Just pick one that you like especially, and cultivate it. Practice turning to it in your mind. Dwell in it until it becomes clear and vivid and real.

Then, when you need to relax, you will have a place to which you always can return for peace.

It will be there. A meadow in the mind is just as tangible and real as any country road can lead you to.

The peaceful valleys that the soul dreams of lie not beyond some far-off range of hills. They are always only in the mind—even if you chance to find them on this earth. It shall not avail you to become a geographer or to study maps, unless you find a map of mind. You rocketeers who make the breathless journey into space, you will not find among the stars the light you seek.

Beyond the blue hills of imagining, no farther than a thought's throw away, fair as a dream of beautiful happenings, joyous as a vision of happy times, there the peaceful valleys lie.

XIX

THE NEED FOR DENIAL

৵ৢ *You stand at the door* ৡ৵

I saw the Master sitting relaxed and tranquil, and I said:

"When I have learned to relax, am I then the master of meditation?"

The Master said, "When you have learned how to use the zero, have you mastered mathematics?"

Then I saw that when you have learned to relax your body so that it is quiet and at rest and your breathing is softly smooth and effortless; when your mind can find its way into the green valley of its own composure, or can lie at peace beside its waterfall of thought and listen to the singing of the bird of truth—you have come far down the road of prayer.

But we all have times when the way is not smooth. Thoughts and feelings arise in us that disturb us.

Doubts flicker across the faith we need.

Fears shatter the composure we are seeking.

We set out for the valley, but we do not get there.

Prayer is a two-sided process as thought and life are a two-sided process.

We all stand at the door of our mind and say Yes and No to every thought that knocks and asks to enter in. Some thoughts do not knock, but slip in when we are not paying close attention; these, too, we let through the door.

This does not mean that by taking thought, we can determine all that will happen to us.

Life comes largely, not out of the conscious part of our nature where we have control and can determine what may go in and come out, but out of the unconscious part of our nature.

What we have in us—thoughts, feelings, desires, needs, fears, hopes, drives—all the complex pattern that our thinking and acting have woven through the entire period the soul has existed —is expressed through us in our body, our mind, our life.

To a great extent, what we already are determines what we will be. To us come continually all sorts of thoughts and feelings, but we draw them in great measure. Like attracts like; what we have let ourselves become draws its own to it. If we have made ourselves a roosting place for starlings, more starlings flock to cackle in our boughs. If we have made ourselves a nesting place for nightingales, yet more nightingales perch singing in our melodious shade.

God made us in His image, and He planted in us the seed of divine life.

The seed took root and grew, and drew to itself the substance of earth and air. Strange birds came and made nests in it. Strange winds shook its leaves. Strange worms gnawed at its root. The rivers that fed it from below and the rains that fed it from above watered it with strange waters.

The tree of your life grew where the seed had found lodgment —out of the rock, or the sidewalk crack, or the fertile valley, or the wood so dense no light trickled down, or the windy grove on the hill.

Because of where it found itself and what happened to it, the tree may have had a stunted or twisted growth, but the tree grew as best it could, seeking always to express the image in which it had been formed.

The tree is you.

And you are the tree of God.

The seed from which you started is a divine seed.

The divine force is still at work in you.

Your soul has to work out what is in it to work out. But you can do what you can. And there is much that you can do.

You can control your conscious thinking.

This you can do.

And there is nothing more important.

For you think—as I have written—thought by thought. There is no other way.

So, thought by thought, you can change your thinking.

Thought by thought—one thought at a time—word by word,

THE NEED FOR DENIAL

deed by deed, we built the life and the soul and the body that we now see in expression.

What we have done, we have done.

But we can change what we are doing now.

We have come up to here. But where we go from here is up to us.

Thought by thought—and only thought by thought—there is no other way—we can change ourselves and our direction now.

To do this, we have two tools. One of these is the power of denial.

The other is the power of affirmation.

We use them, consciously or no.

To every thought that comes to our door, we say, "Yes, yes," or "No, no."

To every thought.

We can deny every life-defeating, joy-defeating, love-defeating thought that seeks entrance into our mind. We can shut the door of our heart to these.

We can affirm life-fulfilling, joy-fulfilling, love-fulfilling thoughts.

⚜ Yes, yes and no, no ⚜

Thoughts come to us.

All sorts of thoughts.

All sorts of feelings.

They all come to the one door, and try to push their way in, or entreat us to let them in, or try to slip in stealthily.

This is the door of our conscious thinking. It is a very narrow door. There is room for only one thought at a time—though a thought or feeling we have repeated many, many times knows the doorway so well and can slide through so quickly that it may slip in almost unobserved while we are giving our attention to some less familiar thought.

But to this door every thought that we have given room to has come. To it every thought comes now. Some of these are thoughts that drag us toward defeat. Some lift us toward victory. But to every one, we have the power to say, "Enter in," or "Stay out."

We have the power of denial.

We have the power of affirmation.

Denial and affirmation—these are the two great processes of mind. These are the two great tools that we can use in changing our life.

We should use them in our moments of prayer and meditation, but we should try to make all our moments a kind of prayer and meditation—because every moment we are denying or affirming something.

Denial and affirmation are the processes by which our mind works; we use them all the time. They are reshaping our life continually.

Affirm or deny, we must.

They are the wings on which our mind takes flight. "I believe," says one. "I do not believe," says the other. Together they drive us toward our goals.

We are constantly affirming or denying—something. Not just when we sit down and fold our hands and say we are praying. Perhaps, least of all then—because sometimes we are just going through motions of prayer—though these are better than nothing at all.

But we are affirming or denying something with every thought we think, every word we speak, every act we do.

Sometimes what we are thinking, saying, and doing is vigorously denying what we tell ourselves we want in our life.

Sometimes what we are thinking, saying, and doing is vigorously affirming what we tell ourselves we do not want in our life.

In the ordinary course of life, we simply affirm what we have come to believe to be true, and we deny what we do not believe. "This is true," we say of something. "This is not true," we say of something else. But we can use these two great tools consciously.

We can deny what is life-defeating to believe.

We can affirm what is life-implementing to believe.

So we can come to a new and higher view of things. We can arrive at a larger, freer truth.

We can change what we think.

We can change what we feel.

We can change what we believe.

We can change our life.

We can do this only a thought at a time, but we can do it a thought at a time.

Every time a thought comes to us that is a life-denying thought, and we deny it room in our mind, we move toward a larger life.

Every time a thought comes to us that is a life-affirming thought, and we affirm its truth and accept it into our mind, we move toward a larger life.

✑ Old familiar faces ✑

To use the process of denial and affirmation to help us become what we wish to become, we deny all life-denying thoughts, we affirm only life-affirming thoughts.

What is a life-denying thought?

What is a life-affirming thought?

Thoughts that keep you from happiness, that hinder you from achieving your potential, that result in hurt to other human beings—these are life-denying.

Thoughts that lead to happiness, that enable you to achieve your potential, that bless other human beings—these are life-affirming.

For myself, I have felt that there are three great basic attitudes that above all others keep us from realizing our potential.

One. We feel unworthy.

Two. We feel inadequate.

Three. We feel unloved.

These three great basic attitudes, above all others, keep us from our good. They keep us from becoming all we might become and they cause us to strike out at others.

It is these feelings—and others of the same ugly ilk—that we should stop at the door of our mind and ask of them, "Why should I let you in?"

Unfortunately, such life-denying thoughts usually disguise themselves so that they can creep by without our suspecting their true nature.

They do not sign a register in our mind as agents of a hostile power.

Feelings of inadequacy do not come and declare, "I have come to paralyze your faith and keep you from doing what you might do."

Feelings of unworthiness do not announce, "I have come to destroy your self-image and debase your soul."

Feelings of unlovedness do not cry out, "I have come to dilute your joys and spoil your relations with your fellows."

They do not come like cloaked and bearded foreigners. They present old familiar faces and they wear gray, everyday clothes.

How, then, shall we sort out friend from enemy? How shall we recognize what we are thinking and know if we are entertaining thoughts and feelings that we should be casting out?

Let us look at some of the disguises life-denying attitudes are likely to wear.

Thus, we feel small and powerless; so we swell and make ourselves look big, as certain fish and lizards and birds do, when we are frightened.

Likewise, we may fawn on people and make ourselves their servants, because we feel unloved.

We walk down a street in the evening when people are turning on the lights in their houses and we look in the lighted windows and feel desolately alone.

We like stories that are sad stories, about the ugly duckling and the little match girl.

We feel that stories that turn out badly are deep and honest, and stories that have happy endings are shallow and contrived; or we refuse to read any story that makes us question life and its meaning.

Our sympathies are always with the outcast and the underdog; or we do not like anyone who is different in any marked way—of different race or color or religion—or indicates he has a different set of values.

We feel uneasy when we have to eat in a snobbish restaurant; or we are only comfortable when we own things that have a fancy label and a high price.

We are reluctant to ask a clerk to show us some goods unless we feel we are going to buy; or we ride roughshod over the feelings of those who have to serve us.

Strangers near us laugh; we look at them with suspicion. Friends do not smile or speak grumpily when they pass us in a hall; we feel on the defensive.

We are driven to join social organizations; or we cannot join any at all.

We are excessively solicitous and constantly overlook our own needs to wait on others; or we are wits and have to make mock of everyone else.

We have to have attention, even if just by coming late when we should be on time or making loud noises when we should be still.

We overdress and spend a great deal of time in front of a mirror; or we pay no attention to neatness at all.

When we have a pain, we imagine it to be a symptom of a dread disease.

We read the headlines in the newspaper and are full of anxiety or anger about the state of the world.

We are uneasy when we see a black cat or walk under a ladder; or we go out of our way to display our disregard of superstitions.

We imagine unpleasant things coming to pass.

We have habits that we cannot control, although we feel we ought to.

Sometimes we feel compelled to go back and try the door, though we locked it; to check the gas, though we are sure we turned it off; or to search the house.

We do not like to be alone in the dark. We are afraid of storms. We have bad dreams.

We cannot relax and have to keep busy all the time; or we always feel tired and cannot concentrate on any task for long.

We collect things and can never throw them away; or we can keep nothing, quickly tiring of our dearest possessions.

We feel an impulse to jump from a high place. We do not like to be in a crowd. We feel uncomfortable in an elevator.

We suffer from nerves or headaches or stomachaches.

All these are ways in which life-denying thoughts and feelings may show themselves.

Every thought that gets in the way of our becoming what we were meant to be; every thought that separates us from our fellow human beings; every thought that increases hatred or fear or ignorance—this is a life-denying thought.

Every thought that frees us to develop and use our powers; every thought that enables us to trust ourselves to life, confident that life can be trusted to bring growth; every thought that increases love and faith and wisdom; every thought that enables us to work to better the human community—this is a life-affirming thought.

✢ Asleep on an anthill ❧

Paul said, "Pray without ceasing."

Is there any other way?

I do not mean that we have to be on our knees without ceasing, or utter affirmations without ceasing.

I do mean that we have to guard our thoughts without ceasing; we have to keep the gateway of our heart without ceasing; we have to be God-ward bent, that is, goodward bent, without ceasing.

We are the sum of our consciousness. All that we have thought and felt and done is expressed in our life now. Life is not a matter of a few minutes a day when we sit down and pray.

We live twenty-four hours a day. All that time we are expressing one thing or another and we are thinking one thing or another. If fifteen minutes a day we are thinking how good God is and putting ourselves in His keeping, and the rest of the time we are thinking how bad the world is and wondering how we are going to stay alive in it, it is easy to see what kind of life we are likely to shape for ourselves.

We are judged, Jesus said, by every idle word.

This is a tremendous statement, and a true one.

We must account for our every thought.

And indeed, we keep account of every thought. Every thought we think becomes part of us and swings the balance toward life or away from it.

Most of our thoughts, considered alone, are not very weighty. But they are never alone. They go into the house of our mind and there they seek out other thoughts like themselves.

And where one thought cannot move us here or there, a whole company of like thoughts may move us where they will—and where we would not!

Thoughts are like ants. A single ant may annoy us, but we can brush it off easily, and it does us no harm. But let us fall asleep on an anthill where a thousand ants have time to swarm over us, and we will wish we had been more careful where we laid ourself down.

Perhaps it is better to say they are like bees; for they may come baring their stings, or they may come bearing honey.

Every thought comes to us, bearing its gift—its drop of nourishment or its drop of poison. It is a very little nourishment and a very little poison—so little that most of the time we do not notice which it is. But little by little we are fed and grow more alive; or little by little we are poisoned and grow less alive.

After a while, too, we grow so used to the poison we are not aware of what it is. It just seems natural and right to think the thoughts we think. We may even grow to like them; and when they are taken away, we may have withdrawal symptoms.

We have become drug addicts, as much as if we took heroin or cocaine, though this drug we are addicted to is merely our own habit of thought.

The life-negating spirit of our thought has become our very own. It does not want to let us go and we do not want to let it go. Without it, we feel empty.

But we can let it go—and we must let it go—if we want to live.

Sooner or later most of us do. Sooner or later most of us look around us, and when we see that the road we have been going down has not brought us where we would go—we find ourselves in a bramble thicket or a pit—we turn around and try to find our way out.

Denial is going back to the fork in the road.

Deliberate, conscious affirmation of life-affirming thought usually is not a continuous process. We set aside times—definite periods—when we sit down and try to realize our oneness with God and life and love and power. We may take life-affirming prayer-statements.

But denial is different from affirmation. Denial, to be truly effective, must be continuous.

We need times for affirmation, but we need to deny all the time.

Socrates said that the unexamined life is not worth living. Unless we have established positive habits of thought, we will soon find that our unexamined thoughts can make life not worth living.

Eternal vigilance is the price of liberty. If this is true in the world of politics, it is even more true in the world of thought. Thoughts follow one another into our mind. We must become conscious of what we are thinking.

If we would become the master of our own thought and master of our own life, we must master one thought at a time.

ᴇᴈ You learned to be you ᴈᴇ

Many of us do not like the idea of denial.

We want to build the building, but we do not want to clear the site.

We like our food to be clean and served on clean plates, but we do not like to wash dishes.

But sooner or later, if we want food, we have to wash the dishes. If we want a new building, we have to call in a bulldozer—or at least, have to pick up a shovel and rake and wheelbarrow.

There is no other way.

Most of us have thoughts, feelings, attitudes that are unprofitable. We continue to have them after we make up our mind not to have them.

We have learned unprofitable ways of thought, unprofitable ways of reacting to events; and we continue to think and react as we have learned to think and react.

We do not stop thinking thoughts that impede our life merely because we decide to. First we have to recognize what they are—and this is not easy. Because they come as mummers in a masquerade. They wear false faces and do not give their real names.

Fear may come looking like bluster, and hate may come looking like fawning. Ignorance may not look like ignorance at all, but like authority and custom and the way things have always been.

But even after we have learned to recognize the thoughts that defeat us and lessen our aliveness, we still continue to think them.

Because we have learned to think them.

We are largely habit.

We see life as we see it because we have learned to look at it that way.

We think the thoughts we think because we have learned to think that way.

We react the way we react because we have learned to react that way.

We like what we like because we have learned to like it; we dislike what we dislike for the same reason.

We want what we want; we dream the dreams we dream; we work the way we work and at the kind of work we work at—because we have learned to do so.

You have learned to be you.

You are a few instincts and a lot of habits.

Most of what you learned to be you did not learn consciously.

But you learned it well. You learned it exceedingly well.

You learned to be you.

How did you learn?

An event occurred. In response to it, you thought certain thoughts and took certain actions.

The same event—or a similar event—occurred again. You had the thoughts you had had before and repeated the actions.

In a short time you did not have to think about the thoughts you were going to think or the action you were going to take.

They were you.

You had become these thoughts and actions.

You had planted a thought and harvested a habit.

You had planted a habit and harvested a nature.

You had planted a nature and harvested a life.

◄§ The bent you want §►

But if you are what you have learned to be, you can become whatever you learn to become.

The life you built thought by thought, you can change thought by thought.

That is the only way you can change it.

That is the way you are changing it, whether you will or not.

You are not a life finished; you are a life in process.

For you are thinking thoughts all the time.

They are fixing you more rigidly in the shape you have formed, or they are changing the shape.

It took you twenty, thirty, or even seventy years to learn to be the you you now are, but you grew the way you grew unconsciously for the most part.

Now you can consciously change the you you have learned to be.

You still grow as you grew before—thought by thought.

But now you can bend every thought—not just an occasional thought—in the direction in which you wish to grow.

Consider how a plant grows.

It grows a cell at a time. Never any other way. A cell at a time. Out at the end of the twig a new cell appears, changing the shape of the plant.

If the plant lives for one hundred years or even one thousand years, it never grows any other way; it grows a cell at a time. If it grow as big as a redwood tree, it grows a cell at a time.

The growth took two directions. The plant grew in obedience to its own inward pattern—in one way if it was a morning glory, in another way if it was an oak.

And the plant grew toward the light.

In obedience to these two directions, the plant grew—one cell at a time.

But when we consciously direct this growth as a skillful gardener does, we can twist and twine the morning glory into almost any shape we want it. And even the oak or pine we can train according to our will—turn it into a bonsai that after a hundred years hardly tops a small tub or send it towering into the sky, its branches shading half an acre.

We can do the same thing for ourselves. For we are our own soul's gardeners. We can water and feed our mind. We can prune where we should prune. We can train where we should train.

For we are growing, constantly growing—thought by thought—more like what we do not want or more like what we do want.

Like the tree, we tend to grow toward the light, for we are children of light; but our growth may have gotten thwarted.

When we consciously take charge of our thought-growth, we can give our boughs the bent we want and grow toward the shape we would like to have.

If we have been growing for years into a shape we do not want, changing the direction of our growth is not going to be easy, especially in the beginning. We are going to have to keep at the task constantly—pruning away the thought-growth we do not want and encouraging the thought-growth we want. For the more we think in any direction, the more we tend to think in that direction.

So, just as we grew in ways we did not want, after a while we find ourselves growing in ways we want.

✑ A *pebble* or two ✎

When you have gotten a branch growing in a certain direction, it tends to keep right on growing in that direction unless you stop it.

You have to stop it and stop it again and again—ruthlessly prune it and keep on pruning it—and you have to encourage other branches to grow in other directions before you can get the tree to grow the way you want it to grow.

Like a tree, you tend to keep on growing in the direction you have been growing in.

When you have become what you do not wish to be, you want to keep on being what you are.

It takes effort to change.

Newton's laws of motion state that a body at rest will continue at rest; if you want it to move, you are going to have to use energy to set it in motion. Once you have set it in motion, it will continue to move in the direction in which it is moving; if you want to change its direction, you have to use energy.

But once set in motion, a body continues to move.

You have to make the greatest effort when it is hardest to make it—in the beginning.

When you start to change yourself and your life, this is when you have to pray without ceasing.

This is when you need eternal vigilance.

An avalanche is not an avalanche when it commences.

One pebble gets dislodged.

It dislodges two more.

They dislodge another half-dozen.

They dislodge a hundred more.

They dislodge—and they dislodge—and they dislodge and then you have the avalanche.

You can stem the avalanche when it is only a pebble or two.

Once you have ten thousand pebbles and a score of boulders rolling down the hillside, run as you may, catching and holding and turning aside, the roaring avalanche runs faster and carries you with it to the bottom of the gully.

Then there is nothing for you to do but gather yourself, aching and bruised, from the rocks and wreckage, and slowly, laboriously make your way back up the hill again.

But the avalanche was at first no more than a dislodged pebble. Stop the pebble and you stop the avalanche.

So it is with habits of thought. You can easily, almost effortlessly stop them when they start. But let them gather headway, and they will drag you where they would have you go, however hard you try to turn them off.

How little it takes to keep a powerful locomotive from moving when it first starts; the least obstruction set upon the track will stop it then. But let it gather power and roar at its full speed down the track, and almost nothing can stop it.

When thoughts that lessen your aliveness begin to move through your head, this is the time to stop them.

Then they are mere pebbles of thought. If you let them run, they will loosen boulders, even cliffsides of destructive thinking, to roar through you and bear you down in an avalanche of negation.

How do you stop them when they start?

There is only one way. You become aware of what you are thinking.

You become aware of the thoughts that are life-fostering and you become aware of the thoughts that are life-negating.

When life-negating thoughts begin, you prune them out.

✑ *Is this true?* ✑

When a life-negating thought begins to seethe in my mind, I examine it.

What more can I do than examine it in the light of my own highest understanding of truth?

I look at it and I ask myself, Is this true?

I look at it as honestly as I am able. I have never felt that it helps me to say of something, "This is not true," when all the time I believe it is. I have never felt that faith requires me to abdicate my intelligence. For one thing, I do not believe I can. My intelligence is going to keep on presenting its views of the matter, whether I accept them or not. So I have to find a way of viewing things that is acceptable to my intelligence.

I look at things as honestly and thoroughly as I can, according to my highest notions of what is true about life, the world, and myself.

I do not try to fool my intelligence; I try to use it—sometimes to lift me to new and higher truths about truth. Is this not perhaps the highest function of intelligence?

Usually when I examine life-negating thoughts, I quickly see that they are just that. They are not actual conditions in my life, they are just my own bodiless imaginings.

Things happen, but they hardly ever happen as they happen in the mind. It is our imagination that seizes hold of us and carries us down into mind's dark underworld of fear and anger and depression.

So I ask myself of things that pass through my mind:

Has this ever happened?

Is this happening?

Will this happen?

Usually my answer to all three of these questions is No. What is in my mind is not an actual happening, but something happening in my imagination.

So I look at it and I say:

"This has never happened.

"This is not happening.

"This is never going to happen.

"God's good is being expressed in my life."

Even if misfortunes occur and I receive a setback or fall ill, I am not going to profit by becoming frightened or depressed. I am not going to profit by letting my imagination dwell on my misfortune and enlarge it.

I am going to consider every situation in my life; I am going to pray and give all my intelligence, faith, and energy to working it out.

But to worry about it, to brood on it and give myself to fantasies about it—what will this avail me? Worry only turns the knife in the wound of events.

I try to ask of every thought,

Is this true?

Is this necessary?

Is this life-supporting? Will it be productive of good for me or anyone else?

Or is this life-negating? Will it produce harm?

Once I have answered these questions as honestly as I can, I am on the way toward handling the thought.

When we are having a hard time handling our thoughts, it may help if we go to a counselor and talk over what we are thinking. We may see a truer reflection of our thoughts in the quiet mirror someone else holds up for us than in the mirror we ourselves hold up, especially when our hands are shaking or we are wringing them.

Perhaps we may even write out our thoughts about our thoughts. Writing out our thoughts may help us to see ourselves more clearly, to see the direction we ought to be taking, to re-direct our thought-forces.

For most of us, the more concrete and exact we make our thought, the easier it is to control it.

When thought circles in the dark of our mind, it is hard to lay hold of. It is like being in a wood at night; what would be no more by daylight than the rustle of leaves or the leap of a rabbit through the brush, can become the descent upon us of evil spirits —ghosts and goblins and demons—in the uncertain dark.

When we reduce these uncertainties, these vague concerns, to spoken words or even further to words on paper, we see them in true perspective, and we can handle them in our thoughts.

I do not say that I entertain only those thoughts that are life-fostering or that I am so much the master of my own thinking that I am conscious of every thought that enters my mind and let none in that I do not want there. I would not even say that I want such a condition.

I do not want to be in control of my thought.

I want God to be in control of my thought.

I want God to be the master of my mind—and of my life. More and more I refer the events of my life to Him.

More and more prayer becomes my way of thought.

More and more I look for His design; I listen for His word. More and more I trust.

I have not arrived, but I am on the way.

Year by year, slowly, I think more life-fostering thoughts, fewer life-negating thoughts; I have less fear, less anger—yes, and less ignorance. I am able to use more and more of my energy to promote my own good and the welfare of others. More and more of me goes into productive achievement; less and less into destructive impulses.

I am able to think about myself less and others more.

I am able to work more for the work's sake rather than for the rewards.

I am able to say more often—and mean it, "Thy will not mine be done."

XX

THE POWER OF AFFIRMATION

◆⟨ *Magic and imagination* ⟩◆

Thinking of prayers as denial and affirmation, I said to the Master:

"What shall I deny?"

The Master said:

"Deny yourself."

Then I saw how the factors that defeat us all have their rise in our self-centeredness.

How shall I feel unworthy unless I first exalt myself and my self-importance?

How shall I feel inadequate when I feel that it is not I but God in me that does the work?

How shall I feel afraid except for myself?

How shall I feel unloved when I have given myself away in love?

So I saw prayer as the practice of going beyond the limits of myself.

I said to the Master,

"What shall I affirm?"

The Master said,

"Affirm God."

I thought about this and what it meant. I saw that when one prays, affirming, one may affirm many things.

And things are what one is most likely to affirm.

Usually when we sit down to pray, we need something, something physical and material. This thing is what we pray for.

We need health, or release from pain, or supply for our needs— a new house, a new job, more success at the job we have, money to pay bills.

We want somebody to change. Perhaps a wife or husband, or our children; or we want someone to like us—or even love us— more than he does.

We may even want something unpleasant to happen to someone.

Whatever we want, we affirm that we have it. We may do this aloud, in words, or we may do it in our mind.

When our prayers plead instead of affirm, we are even more likely to keep them on the level of things.

"Dear God, give me this or that."

"Dear God, I need a hundred dollars to pay the grocery bill."

"Dear God, make my husband quit drinking."

I once heard a man who had been very successful tell about how he prayed. He believed in affirmative prayer; he filled his mind, he said, with whatever it was he wanted.

He told how he got a Cadillac.

First he told himself he had one. He went into his garage and saw the Cadillac parked there. He delighted in its appearance and appointments. He opened the door and sat in it. He took the wheel in his hand. He started the motor. He heard it running, the soft powerful purr. He felt the gentle vibration of its power. He even smelled the car.

"If you want a Cadillac," he said, "go out in your garage and see it, feel it, smell it sitting there. A new car has its own smell. Smell that Cadillac."

After he had done this a few days—he said—there in his garage the Cadillac waited for him, shining and luxurious, smelling as a new Cadillac should.

When the man spoke to us, he was a millionaire. A few months later, I heard he was broke again.

This was several years ago, and since then he may have made another million. Perhaps several times. This man lived for and by things. So he came under the rule and order of things. It is the rule and order of things that they come and go.

In the world of things, things come and go.

Personally, I am certain that there is a great power in the kind of affirmative prayer the man told us to use.

I am not alone in thinking this.

Man has always used this kind of prayer.

This is the magic of prayer. This is the prayer of magic.

Man has always believed in magic. He still does.

Humanity's first artists drew pictures of bison on the walls of their caves. Then in elaborate rites where the hunters saw and heard and felt and smelled the hunted bison, the witch doctor—the magician priest—thrust a painted arrow into the bison's heart. Then the hunters went out to hunt.

The only thing that would have given the prayer of the man affirming the Cadillac in his garage even more magical power would have been to have in his garage a tire from a Cadillac or perhaps a little paint scraped off one, while he prayed.

The priest in the cave undoubtedly had on the skin and head of a bison and the arrows were probably smeared with bison blood.

Man has always tried to force the world to his will.

Someone has said that magic is the activity of the Will-Spirit.

Magic coerces the world, as science does.

✺§ You can run with the Power §✺

Sir James Frazier in the greatest of all books on the anthropology of religions, *The Golden Bough* (which is the mistletoe!), says that magic and science are the same—only magic is science that does not work; if it works, it is science. Naturally, it is a scientist who says this.

For at least twenty-five thousand years man used the science of magic to get his way with the world.

Magic, like science, works from rules. The rule the magician-priest performed his feats by is a rule of mind-action. It is a simple rule: the rule that like calls forth like.

It is perfectly illustrated by the man and his Cadillac. He has the Cadillac in his mind—he senses his Cadillac, he feels he has it, he thinks he has it—and soon the Cadillac is also in the garage.

We may tend to pooh-pooh prayers like this.

But it is hard to pooh-pooh a Cadillac—and this man was driving one.

We tend to pooh-pooh magic. But our ancestors relied on it for more than twenty-five thousand years. Through all that time they tried it—and they believed it worked.

Even if you have a low opinion of your ancestors, it is hard to believe they were stupid enough to be universally fooled for twenty-five thousand years. Whatever else we savage human creatures are, we are practical people, not simpletons. We have had to find ways of meeting a hard and very-present world that makes continual harsh demands on us.

It is impossible for me to believe that we continued to do over and over again for twenty-five thousand years something that never worked.

Oh, no. It worked.

It may not have worked well. But it worked.

It worked well enough for us to do it for twenty-five thousand years—and for a lot of us to be doing it still.

I do not believe it ever worked well. It was like using whale oil lamps, smoky and guttering, for light. But I am not sure that twenty-five thousand years from now, our progeny will think very highly of what now passes for science.

Magic did not work well because it is the attempt of man to impose his self-will on the world—and this is never going to work well, whether we call it magic—as we used to—or science, as we now do.

It will not work because the Will that works through the world is infinitely more powerful than the self-will that works through me, a single individual.

I may learn some aspects of the Will that works through all and use it to gain my own will. But very quickly, the Universal Will restores the balance. It sweeps on in the direction it is going. When I try to run counter to it—in my own direction—it merely sweeps right on, right over me.

Then I go, head over heels, tossed and tumbled in the Universal Will's direction, whether I will or not.

I may inflict my will on the world—but not for long. Unless my will is life's will. Unless my will is love's will. Then everything works to do my will.

I have a choice.

I can run with the Power.

Or I can learn how to use the Power to run against it—but not for long.

The Power that is at work here is very great. What its ends are, I do not know. But they are very good.

The whole world—all the suns and stars and universes and all of us living creatures in the world—roars up the road where this Power moves us.

There is a wind that blows from the very center of being. It blows toward good—more good than we know, more life than we have ever conceived, more power than we have dreamed possible.

The aim of any true science or of any true magic or of any true prayer is to learn what the Universal Will is and to learn the way to align ourselves with it so that this Power works through us—or even more, so that we work for this Power.

Then prayer becomes a science and science becomes a prayer, for they are both concerned with discovering and serving and bringing into expression the sovereign Will that works for good.

Then we are not trying to impose our little self-will on the universe, but to learn what the Great Universal Will is and to bring it forth in our own lives and for the world.

❧ Not to make things so ☙

The purpose of an affirmation is not to make things so. Many people think that when we make an affirmative prayer, we are saying something that is not so in the expectation that our saying it—and especially our saying it over and over will make it so. This is not the case.

Let us consider an affirmation that I often use.

God is in charge.

This is His world.

I am His child.

These are His people.

Now is His time.

My saying, "God is in charge," and, "This is His world," does not make it so.

God is in charge and this is His world. This is the truth. It is true whether I say it or not. It is true whether I know it or not.

My saying it, my knowing it, does not change the truth of it. All that it changes is my awareness of the truth.

The world does not change because I say it is God's world, but I change. My attitude toward the world changes—and probably everything in my world changes.

It makes little difference to the world whether I know it is God's world or not—but what a difference it makes to me! Because every thought I think, every feeling I feel, every word I speak, every action I take will be different when I think it is God's world.

What a different world I will live in!

There will probably not be one moment or one atom of the world that will remain the same.

The world is God's world, whether I know it or not. But my knowing it changes it for me.

So I affirm and re-affirm it, not to change the world, but to change my awareness of it.

My affirmation will not make something true that is not true.

All that prayer ever really changes is my awareness—but this is all it has to change.

When I become aware that this is God's world, what a world I find myself in then!

A world of life, a world of love, a world of growth and achievement, a world where the human child of God can grow to become the divine man!

King's son or woodchopper's?

Why do I repeat affirmations? Is this a kind of magic formula I am working?

No, it is not. At least not for me.

Personally, I repeat affirmations because I have to.

The purpose of the affirmation is to bring me into an awareness of the truth.

"I am God's child," I say. I say it again and again. Not because I am using a magic, but because I need to expand my awareness.

"I believe; help thou mine unbelief," I cry.

I can see that I am God's child.

But I do not think like God's child.

I do not talk like God's child.

I do not act like God's child.

Certainly I do not often live as if I were God's child.

I live more like a woodchopper's son than a king's son.

I have lived like the woodchopper's son so long that I accept this as the natural way to live and cannot give it up.

My mind and emotions have been raised to believe they are a woodchopper's son. Now they have been told they are the king's son. But they are still in a woodchopper's hut. They are still in a woodchopper's world. "Me a king's son! I cannot believe it!" my mind and emotions say.

I have to re-educate my mind and emotions. Until they believe they are the prince, they will not stride like a prince up to the castle gate, put the slughorn to their lips, and blow the challenge for the kingdom.

Prayer is the process of re-educating the mind and emotions.

The best method we have found so far is the same one the advertising men from Madison Avenue have used so successfully.

It is just repetition. Repetition.

That simple. That powerful.

That is the way we came to believe we are the woodchopper's son. Everything and everyone around us has kept repeating to us that we are.

As we have learned it, now we can unlearn it.

We are not, of course, repeating a lie.

It makes a great deal of difference whether what we are repeating is based on truth or not. Sooner or later the lie will be revealed as the lie. If we are not the king's son, we may come to wish we had never claimed that we were. Our sonship may be put to the test.

In ancient Japan, if you claimed to be a Zen master, anyone had the right to walk up to you, whip out his sword and cut off your head. If you were the master, he could not do it. If you were not the master, you should not have said you were.

You are the child of God.

This is not something you are trying to make true.

This is the truth. You are only trying to come into your own. Say the words, "I am a child of God."

What a simple statement, but how infinite its implications.

If we could ever come to believe this simple statement, "I am a child of God"—not just mouth it as a pretty thought, but believe it clear through, with the cells of our body, as it were—as we believe that we have feet or that the earth will hold us up—everything about us would change—ourselves, our lives, our world.

Now we know this truth as we know that a bird flies high overhead, but we do not hold the bird of truth in our hands—or fly with its wings!

But we can work at knowing it.

We get to the farthest destination a step at a time.

So a thought at a time, a prayer at a time, we move closer to awareness of the truth.

The awareness of truth we need is the awareness of the whole man. It is only this that will change our world.

"Ye shall seek me and find me when ye shall search for me with all your heart."

It is not the half-seekers—those who turn aside when the search grows weary and the way grows hard—who will find the Holy Grail or win the kingdom. High goals call for high strivers.

Those who do not taint their dream with lesser dreams; those who do not lose themselves to lesser ends; those who keep the whole man steadfastly in pursuit of their perfection—these will be there at the high close of the quest.

Yet this does not mean—I think—that it is to those who have never gone astray, the Galahads and Parsifals, that the highest prize is given.

The greatest truth-sayer of all indicated that the highest prize is theirs who have had to find their way back from the husks and the swine huts. He told how Love ran out to meet the Prodigal and clasp him to its bosom when he was yet a long way from home.

You are the child of God. You are a king's son.

Know it. Know it as well as you are able. Keep knowing it —even when it seems far from the truth, even when it seems impossible to believe.

Take your step in faith.

Love will take the other steps.

Love will run out to clasp you to itself when you are yet a long way from home.

❧ The Omaha Express ❧

We try to know the truth about ourselves. Sometimes this is not easy.

We have wandered a long way from home.

We have built our habit of negative thinking well.

To change our thinking is going to take some doing.

It is as if you wanted to go to St. Louis. You go down to the train station. You say,

"I am going to St. Louis," and you get on the train.

But the track that leads from the station does not go to St. Louis. It goes to Omaha.

The train runs along the track you built. After a while it pulls into a station. You look out the window and there is a sign.

The sign says, "Omaha."

If you have built your track to Omaha, it is to Omaha your train will take you.

You may call your train The St. Louis Flyer. All the way to Omaha you may say, "I'm going to St. Louis, I'm going to St. Louis, I'm going to St. Louis."

Nevertheless, you go to Omaha.

Do you want to go to St. Louis? You must build a track to St. Louis.

If you have learned to react to life with pain and fear, you are going to continue to have these reactions until you have learned new ones.

Merely saying you are not afraid, you are not sick—merely changing the name of your train—is not going to change the results in your life. You may fool yourself, but you cannot fool life.

To get to happiness and health, you have to tear up the old tracks to fear and illness. This you do by denial.

You have to build a new set of tracks to happiness and health. This you do by affirmation.

◄§ Jackass Bend §►

I live by the Missouri River.

It is a river of many meanders. Much of the time this does not matter. But when a winter of heavy snows is followed by heavy rains in spring, the meandering river cannot carry the great volume of water that rushes down it.

Because of the many twists and turns, the water cannot flow fast enough. It is slowed down, backs up, rises, overflows the riverbanks—and the land is flooded.

One of the worst of these meanders is not far from Kansas City. It is called appropriately Jackass Bend. A few years ago the engineers decided to change the course of the river there. To do this they dug a straight new channel several miles south of the old one. They even built a new bridge across this channel for the road to run on. They called this—appropriately, too—Liberty Bridge.

When they had the new channel dug, they threw a dam across the old channel. The river poured obediently down its new course and has run there smoothly ever since.

Most of us have a few Jackass Bends in the river that is our life. We need a Liberty Bridge or two to take us where we want to go.

We, too, can dig a new channel of thought, and raise our dam across our old habits of thinking. Then, obediently, freely the river of affirmative prayer will take us where we want it to go.

◄§ Life is alive §►

As we work with affirmative prayer, it is well to keep in mind that everything I have said about denial is equally true of affirmation. Everything I have said about life-negating thought is even more true of life-affirming thought. It, too, grows by growing and does by doing. The more we move in the direction of life, the easier it is to move in life's direction.

After a while we find ourselves moving in this direction without taking thought; it has become our way of thought and life.

Once we get the train rolling down the track we want it to

run on, it is hard for us not to go that way. Once we straighten
out the river, it takes us effortlessly where we want to go.

And when we start to move in life's direction, we have life
itself working for us. This is the direction we are meant to move
in. We are meant to live. We are meant to grow ever more alive.

It is easy to get an oak tree to grow tall and straight, even
when it has been stunted and twisted. Once we remove the
obstructions; once we get it started right—the nature of the oak
urges it powerfully upward. We are God's oak.

To change your life, there is nothing that will help you more
than to keep in mind that life is alive.

You can change the course of the river.

You can build a new set of tracks.

Life is alive.

Life is not rigid, fixed, unchanging, and unchangeable.

If you feel that life is rigid and unchangeable, you will treat
it as if it were. Your mind will become rigid in your attitudes
toward it.

When you get to believing that something is unchangeable,
you will not try very hard to change it.

You may give it a tap here and a prod there. Then you will
say, "Just as I thought, it cannot be done."

But if you come to see that life is alive, you will treat it as a
live thing.

Life changes. This is perhaps the truest statement you can
make about life.

Life is aliveness.

It is pliable, shapable; to be worked with and prayed about.

Life gives itself to you, saying,

"Remake me nearer to the heart's desire."

Life seeks only one thing—to be yet more alive.

It is working, striving, writhing in you and in everything to find
a yet more living form.

There are no facts of life, if by facts you mean fixed and rigid
limits beyond which man's spirit cannot venture.

Facts, too, are only faith.

They are just the faith we have come up to so far—they are
what we presently believe as to the way things are and how they
operate.

Tomorrow—do not doubt it!—they will have changed, for we will have acquired new notions about the way things are and how they operate.

The facts are waiting for someone to change them. Someone will change his way of looking at things—he will see things as no one has ever seen them before, see them from a higher perspective—and then everything will change.

He will walk up to the wall and see the way over it or through it or around it that no one has seen before. Or he may see how to roll the wall away. Or he may even see that there is no wall; it was always only a wizard's wall in a spell cast by the magic of believing.

From the beginning of man's climb, Joshuas have confronted Jerichos, and they have marched around and around the high, imposing walls. Then they blew the trumpets of their faith, and the walls came tumbling down.

You look at the world through a habit of thought.

You have learned to be you. You can learn to be more than you.

You can become the master.

Perhaps, the most limiting belief human beings accept is the belief that they are fixed forms—a thing of limits.

You are not an entity; you are a process. You extend through time.

You are alive.

This means that you are changing.

This means that you are growing.

This means that you are becoming.

This means that you are not what you were a moment ago and a moment hence you will be something new.

You are a new you—always.

⤙ To a sardine's head ⤚

What do you accept as true about yourself, your life, and your world?

What do you believe?

The prayer that is based on what you believe, this is the prayer that is answered.

This is the prayer of faith.

In a book about prayer, you might have expected to read much more about faith. Books about prayer usually make faith into a mystifying something hard to understand. They give us definitions like Paul's, "Faith is the substance of things hoped for, the evidence of things not seen." Then we have to define the definition.

Our faith is simply what we accept as true, what we have faith in. Faith is what we believe in—and everything we believe in. This is the prayer that is answered—the prayer we believe in.

This prayer is answered even when we do not make it.

For by our beliefs we live. We stand on them. We step out on them. We depend on them to bear us up. We bet our life on them.

The Japanese say that if you will pray with faith even to a sardine's head, it will grant what you wish.

And will it not—if you pray with faith?

For it is the prayer of faith and only the prayer of faith that is granted. And it is always granted.

It is not what you want to be true.

It is not what you imagine to be true.

It is not enough to wish for something. What a disorderly—even impossible—world it would be if all our wishes were granted! Think about it for a moment and you will see that we can be grateful they are not.

It is not enough to imagine something. We do not get what we imagine, in spite of the man smelling his Cadillac.

The prayer that is answered is the prayer of the whole man, for this is the prayer of faith.

What do you want and imagine and feel and think and accept to be true? What do you expect to see and reason out as right? What do you act on and live by?

It does no good for us to say, "I believe," when we do not believe.

Instead let us face our unbelief and work to increase our belief.

If our reason says, "I am not convinced," let us find reasons for believing.

If our heart says, "I do not feel it," let us give our heart cause for conviction.

Where are you now?

What do you now have faith in?

You have to believe what you are able to believe in now.

You have to start from where you are.

Do not believe that you can fool yourself—or life.

According to your faith it will be done unto you. Not according to what you say you believe, not according to what you would like to believe—but according to what you believe.

⊷ Faith is all the time ⊷

Our mind is active all the time. There is never a moment of our life when we are not thinking and feeling certain things to be true. There is never a moment of our life when we do not have faith—in this or that. It is not just when we read this book that we have faith. It is not just when we are praying that we have faith. We have faith all the time.

What is important is what we have faith in all the time.

This is what makes the difference in our life.

If we accept sickness as natural, we are likely to get sick—until we change our habit of thought and have faith that only health is natural.

If we accept poverty as natural, we are likely to have to endure lack—until we change our habit of thought and have faith that only plenty is natural.

Most of us have considerable faith in the wrong things.

We may have faith that we will fall ill or lose our money.

We may have faith that evil events are going to take place in the world or happen to us.

Usually we do not call this faith.

We call this fear.

But fear is just the opposite side of the coin of faith. Fear is faith—in the wrong things. Fear is faith in the negative side of life.

All of us have faith. That is, all of us have certain things that we think and feel to be true.

But our faith may not be very strong. Certain things we would like to believe in we only half think and feel to be true. We also half think and feel the opposite to be true.

With this kind of half-faith we may live only a half-life. Life has some health in it—and ill health. Life has some prosperity in it—and lack. Life has some happiness in it—and sorrow. Life has some peace in it—and trouble.

And is this not the kind of life we live?

If we have only a half-faith, we have to start with that.

Do we have a little faith that God can help us? We have to start with that little faith.

Faith has power to grow.

Faith is the power to grow.

Jesus said it is like a mustard seed.

Life does not stand still.

The world is not finished.

You are not fixed.

Truth is a look through a window—what window are you looking through? If you believe this is all there is to see, you will never see any more.

But faith is the power to see more—and be more.

If it were not for those who have faith to see beyond what seems, the world would crystallize and harden into a fixed form—and die.

Faith sees things as they seem to be, but always sees yet more.

Faith is never daunted by appearances. Because it does not accept them as necessarily so. It sees through them to the yet more.

Faith is the power to keep our vision on victory even when we are reeling.

Things, thinking, you

Prayer—affirmation—may take many forms.

We may pray for specific things. As I have said, all of us do this at times.

We may pray for the mental equivalent of the thing we want. That is, we pray not that we may have a certain object, but rather that we may have the idea we think stands for it and will bring it to us.

Instead of praying for a thousand dollars, we pray to be shown how we can obtain it.

Instead of praying for our cold in the head to go away, we pray that we may be freed from the hostility or frustration that we feel is responsible for it.

We may ask God to show us what we need to release or do or have in mind to get the thing we want.

Then we work to gain that.

It is probably better to pray for ideas than for things.

But better than praying for specific things or their mental equivalents is praying for our spiritual growth.

We should pray, "More love, Lord!"

We should struggle for more courage.

We should reach out to life in faith that a meaning and purpose run through it and bring our good to us.

We should work to quicken our intelligence.

To grow in spirit, to grow as children of God—this should be the constant aim of our prayers and of all our efforts.

If we pray for things, we may get them—even if then we have to pray to get rid of them, which is sometimes the case. But no matter how many things we get, they count for little unless we get an inward change—a change of spirit.

Life can be meaningful with or without things, but it cannot be meaningful without a rich spirit.

If we change ourselves, the things will not matter—yet I feel sure they will be there.

If we get the inside right, we will get the right outside. It may not be what we want, but it will be right. It will be good. It will bring us fulfillment.

Prayer may change conditions. It will change our ability to meet and handle them.

For when we pray, whether we get what we pray for or not, we get the change in spirit we need to live effectively.

In three worlds

We live in three worlds, over which we have different degrees of control.

Our first world is the world of our thought. Over our thoughts we have control—not so much as we often imagine, but a considerable measure—and we can enlarge it by following the disciplines I have been describing.

Our second world is the world of our body. Over this, too, we seem to have some measure of control—less than we have over our thoughts, but some. Most of the time, we can tell it to rise or lie down or move an arm or leg, and it will do what we say.

But over most of its processes we have no conscious control at all. Of most of its processes we are ignorant! It is almost as if we were inhabitants of a land whose language we have never learned.

Even over the body-processes we are conscious of, we have little control. Too often we do not tell our body what it will do, it tells us what we will do.

Our third world is our external environment. The world beyond our fingertips.

Here we seem to have very little control. If we want to change it, we feel we have to take tools and attack it with some kind of physical force.

Obviously we have more power over our thoughts than we do over our body and more power over our body than we do over our world.

Because this is so, I feel we should put first things first.

Let us work with our thoughts, which we can control.

Having gained control of ourselves, we may find that we have gained control of our body and external world, too. It is obvious that we cannot work with what we do not have. Let us start with the control we have and go on from there.

⤳ The miracle of myself ⤶

The true end of prayer is not to develop a power to work miracles, but to develop.

I am myself the miracle; if I let myself develop into what I was made to be, I shall find myself with unique powers and extraordinary capacities.

The true end of prayer is to eliminate the mental and emotional factors that bring me to defeat; it is to develop the mental and emotional factors that bring me to fulfillment.

So I pray to keep my vision on perfection and my hands at work bringing it forth.

I pray to have a heart at peace and a mind in ferment. I would be free from anxiety, but constantly spurred to activity.

I would be temperate in everything except enthusiasm.

I would have courage and the faith that makes courage unnecessary. I would be thankful and expectant.

I would be more loving—out of strength, not out of weakness.

I would be in charge of my own thinking so that I can place my thinking under God's charge.

This is the end of prayer—to give me power to do everything I need to do in order to let the power that does all work through me and for me.

I walk into a room and press the electric switch.

Prayer is pressing the switch and having the lights come on.

But prayer is also establishing the connections. By prayer I build the circuit. By prayer I keep the contact. By prayer I use the power in right and good ways so that I do not blow the fuses or burn out the wires.

The dynamos turn forever. But they turn for me only as I connect myself with them and use their power.

Prayer is the power that links me with the central source of power.

◆§ A tale of an elephant §◆

"All is God," declared the Hindu guru. "And God is the infinite, the one, the only, without limitations, without attributes. This is the essence of the wisdom of the ages. This is the beginning and the end of truth."

The student, sitting at the feet of his master, drank in the words in all their heady essence.

"I understand," he exclaimed, "God only is real, and reality is only God. God is one and God is perfect, unaffected by external circumstance. He is everything that is. He is the reality within me. He is the reality within you. All things are only the forms through which He expresses Himself."

As the student left his teacher and walked down the road,

the truth that he had just imbibed seemed so real to him that he felt intoxicated. In the flowers by the roadside, in the beasts in the fields, in the birds that flew overhead, in the human beings who passed by, the student saw only God.

Absorbed in this sweet bliss of divine illumination, suddenly he saw, coming down the road, an elephant. As the huge beast lumbered swiftly toward him, the student could hear the tinkling of the many bells that dangled from its harness. He could hear the soft thud of its great feet on the road. He could hear the voice of the elephant driver perched on its neck, who shouted, "Clear the way! Clear the way!"

But the student thought, "Why should I get out of the way of this elephant? I am God. The elephant is God. Should God be afraid of God?"

Full of faith and without fear, the student kept to the middle of the road. But when God came to God, the elephant, at a command from the driver, with a quick twist of his trunk hurled the student headlong into the ditch.

After a while, dirty, bruised, and shaken—even more shaken in mind than in body—the student crawled onto the road, limped back to his teacher, and poured out his tale of pain and doubt.

"Ah," said the teacher when he had heard the student through, "you are God. The elephant is also God. But why did you not listen when you heard God's voice calling to you from the driver, who is also God, to get out of the way?"

The Hindus tell this story to illustrate the mystery of what is real and what is appearance.

But the story has a point that the Hindus have overlooked. There is one person in the story who was in charge of the situation. When he spoke to the elephant, the elephant obeyed. Had he said, "Turn aside," the elephant would have turned aside. Had he said, "Halt," the elephant would have halted.

This person was the mahout, the elephant driver.

✺ Are you in the driver's seat? ✺

Many of us are like the student. We study God's nature and ours a little while, learn some heady phrases, catch a new insight into reality, and are wafted as on ethereal breezes through the celestial realms of divine metaphysics.

Suddenly we are confronted with an elephant.

We may say some prayers. We may repeat some affirmations. But sometimes, shaken and bewildered, we have to pick ourselves up out of the ditch.

Then we may go back to our books, or to our teacher, or even to God, and in a sense demand, "If all is in God and God is in all, where were you?" Or we may shrug our shoulders in chagrin and dismiss the new truths we have learned about life with the thoughts, "It doesn't work. The elephant won't obey."

But the elephant does obey. It obeys the one who is in the driver's seat. It will not do what we want it to do because we think lofty thoughts or speak magic phrases. It will not turn aside because we are mystics or because we are good people morally. It will not kneel because we have absorbed the contents of a book on metaphysics. But when we have established our authority over it, it will obey us, not because we compel it, but because its very nature—the very nature of the universe—compels it.

The student was not wrong in his insight into the nature of things or in his faith that he did not have to be afraid of the elephant. He was wrong in not realizing that before he could master the elephant he had to become the master.

◆§ While waiting for a bus §◆

Some of us would like to command the elephant when we have not yet learned how to make even our little dog obey.

If we cannot discipline ourself, we will never be able to discipline our dog.

Our dog cannot respond to discipline we cannot give.

Can we say to ourself, "Stay!" and stay?

Can we say to ourself, "Go!" and go?

When we are able to obey, we are in command.

I do not believe we have dominion over anything we are not superior to.

"I will transport myself through the mysteries of life and death," we think—and we have not yet gained enough mastery to keep from being bored on a rainy Sunday afternoon.

We would command the rain to stop, and we are still afraid of getting wet.

Let us rise in thought above the rain where we are able to have a happy time, rain or no rain—interestingly, if we rise high enough even in the outer world we rise above the clouds and rain —and we may find it stops.

At least, we are above it.

"I will make the forces of heaven and earth conform to my will," we declare—and we cannot keep from feeling irritated if the bus is five minutes late.

I have often thought that a book on prayer should be entitled, "How to Be Happy While Waiting for the Bus."

For I feel certain we cannot hope to have power over things as long as things have power over us.

All of us must confront the elephant. The world and life come thundering down the road of time. Some men turn aside. Some are tossed into the ditch. But some master the elephant. These it lifts onto its neck and bears triumphant to their destination.

✺§ Of discipline and mastery §✺

How do we get into the driver's seat?

If we would have the elephant take us where we would go, we must master the art of driving the elephant. It is man's destiny— I believe—to become a master of heaven and earth and life and death—but we must earn this mastery.

How do we get the great beast that is the world and life—but is also the expression of God as we are the expression of God— to kneel down and let us mount upon its neck and bear us wherever we would go?

Some time ago there were two pictures on the front page of my newspaper. One picture showed a famous lion tamer in the ring with a lion; the lion, fangs bared, was slowly backing away from him. The story told how this man, cracking a whip, firing blanks, prodding with a chair, made his lions do what he wanted them to do; it also told how he had been mauled several times.

The other picture showed a young man asleep in bed beside a sleeping lion. The story told how the young man had raised this lion from a cub. Now he had been drafted by the Army and the lion he had had to leave behind him was wasting away for the love of its master.

Many men, like the lion tamer, rely on force. And often they succeed. Through brute strength and weapons, they simply overpower what they exert their energies against—an elephant, a lion, a disease germ, a man, or a nation of men. But force wins only uneasy victories. For force always calls forth force. The victory that comes out of force depends on force for its keeping. He whose mastery of an elephant depends on force is wise to have learned to sleep lightly.

And there are areas where force does not work at all. Force works mainly on things. In solving an algebra problem, for example, it is of no value; it cannot prove a quadratic equation. Confronted by spiritual needs, it is helpless; it cannot make me loving nor can it make another love me.

We rely on force because we sense that mastery in any field is largely a matter of obtaining authority. But authority is a very intangible matter. It is based on faith and intelligence more than on force.

Sometimes, of course, it wears a uniform or has a sign over its door that says, "Very Important Person." But true authority does not have to be accompanied by a police escort; it does not have to crackle commands.

Authority may be a still small voice. Perhaps it just says, "Yes, I can do that." Or perhaps, "This is the way." Or even, "I am the way." Perhaps, it just does what has to be done without saying anything at all.

Jesus acted from authority; He knew that He was the master. He knew this when He went to the wedding feast at Cana. He knew this as He walked toward the pool of Bethesda. He knew this as He stood outside the tomb near Bethany, where Lazarus was three days dead. He knew this as He toiled up Calvary.

When we meet a man in authority, we sense that he has a deep abiding inward trust and the courage to step forth on his trust and do what has to be done by him. And we catch his trust from him.

This is why the elephant kneels down to the mahout, not because of force.

How do we attain this trust and courage?

I watch a friend play a sonata by Beethoven. His hands flash over the keys and perfect harmonies pour forth. The music bubbles, whispers, thunders at his touch. And all the while he plays, my friend is talking to me about metaphysics. "How easily you play," I say. And so he does. But how much exercise of intelligent discipline went into that easy mastery!

As I have said, there is a discipline of prayer and a prayer of discipline.

Authority comes out of intelligent discipline.

At first thought, discipline may seem like something disagreeable. But discipline does not have to be hard. At best it is a labor of love; we do not have to be made to do what we want to do. No one had to force my friend to sit at the piano eight hours a day; sometimes someone was needed to pry him away from it.

But easy or hard, willing or unwilling, if we would be the master, we must accept discipline. And the discipline we establish must be over ourselves before it can be over anything else. The elephant cannot respond to discipline we cannot give. Before we can make life obey us, we must ourselves learn to obey. When we are able to obey, we are in command.

And we must never give up. We must be willing to go on as long as we have to go on to get where we set out to go.

Mastery is not a matter of time. Sometimes it comes on the first effort; sometimes, on the thousandth effort.

⋙ When we love ⋘

When we love what we are doing, it is no effort to keep on doing it. This is why, if we would master prayer, we need to pray in love and love to pray. The prayer we make for ourself, as much as the prayer we make for another, needs to be a prayer of love.

I doubt if we ever truly master anything we do not love—whether it be a skill, a fortune, our own body and mind, an organization, an art, a science, a people, or an elephant.

But most of us rely on love only occasionally. We do not have much faith that love will work—except on those who love us, our wife, or our child, or our friend. We have not come to the place where we see that the whole universe is the work of love. Yet such it is. The tonic chord to which creation vibrates is the chord of love. When we strike it, there is nothing in the world that does not vibrate in sympathy.

Love brings the beast to its knees, not through fear and force, but out of the urge to love and be loved that moves the universe. When love is in the driver's seat, love is the beast that is driven. There is neither driver nor driven; they are of one mind—the Mind of God, who is love. One does not want to go where the other does not want to lead him.

Love is identification. I do not have to order my ears to hear nor my heart to beat. My ears hear and my heart beats—not because I order them, but because they are identified with me. Love foresees commands and supplies needs before the need is spoken.

I will not have to impose my will on another when we both are seeking to carry out the wisdom of God. I will not have to command another when we both are listening for the prompting of love. I will not have to impose my will on life; for life will become not a coercion but a co-operation, a joyous enterprise in which every atom of creation shares; not one will be left out.

This is what the Master who was love incarnate came to show us: Life waits to give itself to us—its powers and its treasures— when we give ourselves in love. When we give ourselves in love, love with a few loaves and fishes feeds a multitude, heals a leper, gives back sight to a blind man, and in a matchless hour of giving even every remnant of self, rises triumphant over death and rolls away the stone from the tomb of all the sons of man.

The day must come when like the student in the story we will be going down the road and toward us will thunder the elephant. And we shall have only love and faith in our love. And we shall see, as the student tried to see, that it is not a beast that rushes upon us, but love. And love will kneel before us and lift us onto its back and bear us wherever we may wish to go. And we shall look about us, and all that we shall see is love.

XXI

HOW ANSWERS COME

❧ We grow accustomed ❧

I said to the Master,

"How long will it take me to change myself, my life, and my world?"

The Master said,

"How long *did* it take you?"

I saw that changing my thoughts and feelings about life, learning to see it in different terms, even love's terms, and living on different terms, is not a question of time—but it may take time.

How long did it take me to dig the pit?

It may take time to dig out of it.

If I have learned life-negating habits of thought, I may tend to cling to them, the way I cling to old shoes or an old hat.

I am comfortable in them—even when they are uncomfortable—and I feel naked and uneasy when I give them up.

I am like the little boy who carries everywhere the old tattered blanket from the crib where he no longer sleeps.

We get used to anything after a time and are not at ease without it.

We become as used to being bound as we are to freedom. Let the tiger born in the zoo cage find his way into the open fields, and he is not elated; he is bewildered.

We are like the man who has slept on a hard floor all his life; when at last he can buy a bed, he cannot fall asleep in it.

Many men find unaccustomed riches harder to bear than their familiar poverty was.

We grow accustomed to our way of life, our way of looking at things—even when it is a painful way—and we do not want to change it.

"This is the right way, the true way," we cry.

In the country of the blind, when one man receives his sight and begins to tell his fellow countrymen what things are like, they do not thank him for bringing them the light; they curse him for corrupting truth.

New truths are reluctantly accepted—perhaps most reluctantly of all by those who consider themselves to be the keepers and interpreters of truth.

✌ Hercules and the Hydra ∂≈

When people ask for prayers, they may ask for many things. "Change my life," they may cry. "Change my job, or the condition of my health, or my wife, or give me some new friends, or a new heart, or a new bank account."

But how rarely they cry, "Change me. Change my thinking."

Yet this is all they can change. For men have power over nothing in this world except over their own thoughts.

But this is all they need to change.

When they change their thinking, they change the center from which everything else is viewed and takes its form.

Negation is like the Hydra Hercules had to destroy. It had nine heads; every time Hercules cut one head off, he found two more heads growing in its place. As long as Hercules kept hacking away at the heads, he had no power over the Hydra.

The life-negating thoughts we wrestle with have many heads.

We isolate one of our fears. We reason and work with it, and at last we see that it serves no good purpose in our life and has no reasonable basis in fact.

"Off with your head, false fear!" we cry and lop it off. Then we turn around, and there are two more fears grinning their evil grin at us.

Cutting out each separate life-negating thought is an everlasting process and keeps us running to and fro in an agony of anxiety all our life.

We have to realize that we have to destroy, not the heads, but the whole beast, the source from which they draw their sustenance.

This source is our basic attitude toward ourself, our life, and our world.

As long as this is negative, we shall be surrounded by ugly heads snarling and snapping at us.

So long as we feel we are unworthy, inadequate and unloved, this central falsehood on which we base our thought about ourself, our world, and our life will spawn a horde of false fears.

It is like trying to get rid of bindweed by pruning away its tendrils. The great root of the plant lies hidden underground, and we must get rid of the root if we hope to get rid of the flowers.

Continue to think you are unloved, and that thought will put forth ten thousand stems and leaves and flowers and seeds.

Continue to feel inadequate and unworthy, and false fears will never cease to bind and thwart your potentialities for productive living.

Pinch off one fear; it has already formed two others.

But come to realize that you are not unloved, you are the beloved child of God; come to know that you are not inadequate, you are the capable child of God; come to feel that you are not unworthy, you are the perfect child of God—and the bindweed that clotted your life—all the twisted stems and throttling leaves of fear and hate and misery that kept you from your happy flowering—will have withered away.

How far from home are you?

How long are you going to have to pray to see results?

If you were drowning and began to breathe again, how many breaths would you have to take before you had results?

It is with prayer as with breathing.

Every breath you breathe brings results.

Every prayer you make brings results.

You are thinking all the time.

You are having thoughts about yourself, about life, about your world and all the things and people in it.

Each of your thoughts is affirming life or denying it.

Each thought is moving you toward health, success, happiness, a unified active self. Or it is moving you in the opposite direction away from what you hope to achieve.

What are you thinking now?

Only you know what is passing through your mind.

Is it life-implementing?

Is it helping you to meet effectively the things you are having to meet?

Is it making you happy?

You may need no affirmations to turn your thoughts in a profitable direction. You may need one. You may need ten thousand and one.

Only you can know.

How many steps do you have to take to get home?

It depends on how far from home you are when you turn your heart toward home again.

~§ This one thing I do §~

The answer to prayer comes as a creative act.

The answer to prayer comes!

We do not bring about the answer to our prayers. God answers prayer.

We have power over only ourselves. God has power over everything else.

Someone has said, "Those who want to be gods have failed at being merely human."

It has rained at picnics I have attended. I have prayed for things I have not gotten.

But then I do not believe that the universe was made for the gratification of my wishes. The universe was arranged not to make my fondest dreams come true but to make truth my fondest dream.

The universe was made, not to do my will, but to do the will of its Maker—and so was I.

When I do this, my good will come to me.

I wish I knew a magic prayer that would guarantee your wishes against frustration. I wish I could say: "If you will just do thus-and-so, you will never have another ache or trouble."

All I can say is this: If you will do what I suggest in this book, you will grow. You will grow in your power to handle effectively the conditions of your life.

I know that prayer works.

I have seen it work.

I have seen people healed.

I have seen people receive asked-for supply in such astonishing ways that those who saw it could only exclaim, "A miracle!"

I have seen many prayers answered, and a single answered prayer proves that there is a power that answers prayer.

I know with no shade of doubting that as we change our habits of thought—eliminate the mental and emotional factors that defeat us and develop the mental factors that bring us to fulfillment —our life changes and blossoms in ways we can scarcely believe.

But the human being is a complex creature in a complex world.

I am a human being. I have come up to where I am. As long as I am human, I come under the laws and conditions that govern human beings.

As a human being, I have only a part-view of things. I do not always know my good.

But one thing I do know is good: It is good to pray and keep on praying. The fact things do not always turn out the way I want does not release me from the necessity of ordering my thoughts.

I will pray about everything that comes into my life.

I will pray in small events and large events. I will pray in troubled times and happy times. I will pray concerning easy things and hard things.

I will pray and keep on praying. I will not give up. If I have to pray for the impossible, I will pray for that.

Thought by thought I will press on in prayer.

Like Paul, "I count not myself to have apprehended; but this one thing I do, forgetting those things which are behind, and reaching forth unto those things which are before, I press toward the mark for the prize."

I may not be where I want to be. I may not be where I will be. But I am not where I was.

How long does it take for prayer to be answered?

It does not take time at all.

It takes uniting yourself with God so that His power can work through you.

This comes only out of praying.

❦ To master the instrument ❧

When we learn to play the piano, we are not surprised to find that it takes many years of diligent practice every day. To play certain passages, we have to practice them hundreds, thousands, perhaps hundreds of thousands of times. We accept this as part of learning to play. Even then, with years of daily practice, most of us do not master the instrument.

Likewise, when we set out to write, we accept the fact that we may have to practice writing for years before we can write well. Even after years, sometimes to produce ten lines of acceptable verse we have to write fifty—even a hundred—pages that are unacceptable. But if we want to write well, we are willing to do this.

But to become masters of prayer, we pray a few times and seeing no results, give up, saying, "Prayer does not work."

Yet how much more the art of prayer needs to be practiced than the pianist's or the poet's art! The human soul is intricate, strange, elusive, contradictory, subtle, full of forces we do not understand, alive with appetites, hopes, fears, dreams.

And this soul is the instrument we must learn to play if we would master prayer.

We should not count on the answer to prayer taking time, but we have to be willing to give it all the time it takes. There is no knowing how much time it will take.

The answer to prayer comes in the same way all creative acts come.

We pray and work, and there is no visible sign that anything is taking place. Then one day, of a sudden, the process is complete and the answer to our prayer comes forth.

This may be the way it sometimes is at Lourdes. Most of the sick who go to Lourdes go after they have tried everything else. They have done all they could with doctors and medicine; they have prayed and prayed. Sometimes this has gone on for months, even years. Many others have prayed with them. Then they go to Lourdes. And there, in an hour, almost unexpectedly, the healing takes place and the human being is whole.

This is often the way it is with those who turn to Silent Unity. Many, many times we receive word from those who write to us, saying, "You could not have had time to receive my letter—I had scarcely gotten it in the mail—before the answer to my prayer appeared."

But what a work in the invisible has preceded the appearance in the outer.

The answer to prayer comes like this in a sense, whether it appears altogether and at once, or little by little, slowly over a long time. All creative acts take place like this. This is because we do not make them happen. They happen to us—and through us.

God makes creative acts happen.

Only life can bring forth a child or a flower—or an answer to prayer.

Whether the answer to prayer comes whole, taking one prayer to produce a prodigious answer, or whether it comes piecemeal, little by little, taking ten thousand prayers to produce a very little answer—nevertheless it comes to us and through us.

We have to make ourselves a receptive vessel. Then we have to let the answer come. The light is from on high, whether it comes as lightning, in flashes and by fits and starts, or comes as the steady glowing of the dawn.

God—God only—answers prayer.

◄§ A tree to grow §►

Sometimes I wonder if life ever answers prayer except with a seed.

Life never gives us a life lived, but always a life to be lived.

Life never makes a tree grown but a tree to grow.

Life never brings forth a man in the full flush of his powers and deeds, but a babe with powers all to be discovered and deeds all to be done.

Life forms an egg, an embryo, a seed. I see nothing come into being any other way.

Even a hurricane begins as a little spiraling breeze somewhere— and grows.

I have a feeling that the sun did not suddenly blossom forth as the blazing sun we know, but a star-seed blew into space from the tree of light, found a crack in vastness where it could lodge itself, sent forth its root of radiance and leaves of fire, and began to grow.

Healing is not a sudden convulsion of being. It comes cell by cell when the seed of wholeness is lodged in the flesh. Sometimes it makes a morning-glory growth; sometimes it grows as slowly as a bristlecone pine, but always it grows.

Sometimes we are not aware of the growth because it has been going on in the invisible. Then suddenly the invisible flashes into visibility.

Growth is no less real because it takes place in the invisible. Perhaps most of the growth of the world and most of the work of the world is done on the invisible side of things, like the growth of a child in its mother's womb. How far the roots of trees spread underground, so that one fine spring morning, we may exclaim, "Oh, look at all the lovely flowers." It was cell by cell that the growth went on to burst forth in such sudden blossoming. It is thought by thought and prayer by prayer that the change goes on in you. Every thought you think, every prayer you make moves you closer to the flowering of your good.

I look—and I see nothing but things growing.

I see some growing more alive; I see some growing less alive. But always growth.

I see nothing coming into being any other way.

I see life scattering its seeds—star-seeds and petunia dust, redwood seeds and eggs of ants, and man-seeds.

I see life following the order of being—and the order of being creates only seeds.

Nothing is ever finished; everything is to grow. Nothing is ever completed, though everything is complete.

The tree is in the seed; the universe is in the seed. All there. All complete. But it has to become the universe it was created to be.

◄§ His answer is a seed §►

What are you praying for?
I believe God gives us the seed of healing.
I believe God gives us the seed of prosperity.
I believe God gives us the seed of happiness.

What does a healing-seed look like? I imagine it looks like any other seed, full of healing-chromosomes, genes of healing.

Chromosomes are the most essential part of a living cell. They determine what the living creature will grow to be like. They were in the germ-cell from which you started, the cell in your mother's womb—half of them came from your mother and half were brought by your father—and as you grew, these chromosomes have been in every cell of your body. The interesting thing is this: no matter how different different cells in your body look—whether they are white blood corpuscles, capable of assuming almost any shape; or perfectly round red blood cells; or nerve cells with long, whip-like extensions—in all your different cells the chromosomes are always exactly the same. Chromosomes are made up of particles we call genes; each of these particles determine some of your characteristics—whether you have blue eyes or brown, blond hair or black, or whether you are a man or woman.

Do you know what a chromosome looks like? The scientists have looked with their microscopes and they tell us they are spiral-shaped.

This is the way they ought to be shaped.

Chromosomes are only twists in the right direction, in the direction of life. Healing genes are starts of healing. But the tree of healing grows from them.

Likewise, God does not give us prosperity complete. He does not lay some vast treasure at our feet. We do not wake in the morning to find under our pillow a new bankbook showing that a million dollars has been deposited to our account.

But we may wake in the morning with a seed-idea of prosperity, a seed-thought from which uncounted millions may materialize.

We may wake in the morning with a faith that we can achieve success, with a will to be up and after our success, with a determination and a joy-in-effort from which riches unimaginable will spring.

God gives us a power to love and a power to be lovable. God gives us a power to be ourselves and a power to help others to be themselves—and when we let these powers develop and grow, a whole life of happiness may come into being.

All too often when we pray, I think we are looking for the wrong kind of results. We expect a whole organ suddenly to be where a sick organ was; we expect a million dollars to appear in our hands; we expect some extraordinary human being to come up to us in the street and declare, "I love you, you wonderful person!"

But I see nothing in life that would make me think this is the way life works.

Even oaks start as seeds; even elephants. A single cell divides and becomes two; and the two become four; and the four become eight; and the eight become eight trillion perhaps!

Even the mightiest river began as a spring. And even the freest-flowing spring began somewhere as a single raindrop that fell into a crack of the earth and found lodgment where other raindrops could unite with it until at last a spring gushed forth.

I believe life responds to every prayer. But it responds as life responds to every demand on it. Life's response is a seed.

There it is. A life-seed. A seed-thought of health lodged in our flesh. A seed-thought of success lodged in our will. A seed-thought of love and joy lodged in our heart and mind.

If we till and weed and nurture and water and work, that seed will grow. It will grow to become what it was made to be.

Are you praying?

All about you seeds are blowing. Through your mind. Through your thoughts. Through your flesh.

Health will find lodgment in you if you give it lodgment. It will grow into the tree of health, and its leaves will be life.

Prosperity will find lodgment in you if you give it lodgment. It will grow to be a tree of prosperity, and it will bear the fruit that is both riches and honor.

Love will find lodgment in you if you give it lodgment. It will grow to be a tree of love, and the bluebird that is happiness will fly to you and build its nest among your boughs.

God answers every prayer.

But His answer is a seed.

Let His seed grow in you—and you may grow to be even a god.

⋞ *A method of prayer* ⋟

How then shall you pray?

I have told you to start where you are and pray as you can.

If you have no method of prayer, follow the simple method I have given you.

Every day set aside a definite period as your appointment with God—once, twice, as often as you can, but not so often you will not keep it—for a definite length of time—ten minutes, thirty minutes, as long as you can, but not so long you will not stay at it.

During your daily periods of prayer, get as still in body as you can—practice relaxing. Get as still in mind as you can—practice tranquil thinking. Deliberately, consciously fix your mind on life-implementing thoughts. Form them into affirmations. Repeat these over and over, silently if you must, aloud if you can.

Also, realize that every thought you think every moment is a prayer, whether you are formally praying or not. Do not let your thought rule you; rule your thought. Teach yourself to guard your mind. Let no life-depleting thoughts enter in; if they do, turn them into life-implementing thoughts.

In your God-appointment, make your prayers God-pointed. Think how you are one with God. Affirm how you are one with God. Feel how you are one with God.

Feel God's power; feel it working in you.

Feel God's love; feel it enfolding you.

Let God do God's perfect work. Let God.

Look that you may see.

Listen that you may hear.

Reach that you may touch.

For whatever your prayer is, it will be more, if you pray.

Is your prayer no more than a few moments on your knees, crying, "God! God!"

One day prayer will lift you from your knees and send you out to climb the hills of thought. You will fall on your knees there, too; around mind's crystal summit such winds of truth are blowing none can stand.

Does your prayer seem no more than a little candle that you carry in your cupped hands against the winds of the world and blow with the breath of your faith to keep the flame alive?

From it you may yourself catch fire and become a living candle. By your little light someone may find his way through a dark night of the soul.

When you reach out in prayer, do you touch but the hem of reality's robe?

This is enough for now.

He who wears the robe is love.

XXII

THE SEARCH FOR THE INFINITE

❧ On a sunlit morning ☙

We look, but not for a vision.

We listen, but not for a voice.

Prayer—at its best—is not so much a seeking as becoming aware.

Most of the time, when we pray, we do not expect a specific answer.

No great new illumination flashes on our mind.

No healing current gushes through our body.

No splendid idea comes to us that will make our fortune.

We do not suddenly have some deep desire of our heart fulfilled.

But we open the windows and doors of our soul.

We fling ourselves open to that which words are feeble to describe.

Nothing that I can tell you about happens.

If you ask me, I cannot say, "This is new and different. I received this or that."

Nothing happens, yet everything happens.

What happens when you throw open the windows and doors of your house on a sunlit morning?

We do not open our house because we expect anyone to come in.

If I asked you, you might say you were letting the outside in— or spring—or morning. But it might be even truer to say you were letting the inside out.

Nothing changes, yet everything is changed.

The house is not moved.

The rooms are not remodeled.

The furniture is not repaired.

You look the same as you did a moment before.

Yet nothing remains the same.

You are altered in your inmost essence, and you will not ever be the same again.

And you know it, at least for a time.

You put your head out the window or you step out the door, and you breathe the air, and there is not a cell of your body that does not stir with new life—nor a recess of your mind.

There is not a dingy corner of the farthest room that does not take on a different look.

I look at you and may see no change.

I ask you and you cannot tell me how you have changed.

Yet there is no particle of you that is not changed and renewed.

There is no thought or feeling that has not been lifted up.

Prayer is giving yourself to the glory of life.

Prayer is like taking a deep breath.

Prayer is like drinking water when you are thirsty.

Prayer is like standing on a hilltop.

Prayer is like sitting quietly in a deep wood or by a running stream.

Prayer is like being with someone you love.

Prayer is not anything changing, but everything changed.

Prayer may not change anything specifically, but it changes everything essentially because it changes the inmost essence of you.

Prayer opens you to union with the essence of things and the central truth of livingness.

Prayer throws open the windows and doors of your soul. You look out, and breathe in, and stand for a moment still; you let all that is pour in upon all you are, and you let all you are pour out upon all that is.

After that, you turn back to your familiar tasks and nothing at all has changed, yet nothing at all will ever be the same again.

⊸§ A cupful of Infinity §⊷

Is this not the pinnacle of prayer—to fling yourself down before the mystery and to cry out with awe, "My Lord and my God!"

Then having climbed to the topmost reach of mind, alone with Infinity, to feel Infinity bend and lift you to itself, and whisper in your ear, "My son, O my son!"

Then you find that Infinity is not nothing but everything.

You find that the mystery is not mysterious, but a light, and that the light shines for you and in you.

You find that the Infinite is not vast and impersonal, but a heart, and that the heart beats for you.

You find that the Infinite is a Mind, and that the mind is your own.

You find that God is not strange or a stranger, but as close as your own breath and as near as your own thought.

You find that, having gone beyond God as a person, you come to the Person of God.

Not a person as you and I are persons—but Intelligence and Love, a Mind that thinks and a Heart that feels.

It is not right to think of God as a person, to make God in my image.

But when I go beyond the idea of God as a person, let me not make Him less than a person.

I am a person—shall I make God less than I am?

No, God is not less than a person; God is more than a person.

He is all that I mean when I speak of a person—and yet an infinity beyond.

As a person, I am contained within my personal limitations.

God also has His limits as a person, but He contains them.

He knows what it is to be a person—to be born and die, to have needs and desires, to suffer and be afraid, to love and hate, to live and grow.

He knows what it is to be finite me, as the tree knows what it is to be a root or a leaf.

But the tree is more than its root or leaf, and God is more than His finite me.

When God goes beyond His limits as a person, what is He then?

I have no need to say except to know that though the Infinite is beyond all that I can say of it, it is never more love than I can bear, more wisdom than I can grasp.

The Infinite is not cold, vast, distant, inaccessible, but as warm and close as love, as intimate as thought.

What endless oceans water is, but it is also these trembling and transparent drops I pour from my cup and drink to quench my thirst! Water takes the shape my cup gives it, but there is more to water than this cupful.

What an endless sea the air is, but it is also the breath that I breathe in and out! Air becomes the breath my lips form, but there is more to air than this mouthful.

God is a power beyond my power, yet a power that works through my powers.

God is a mind beyond my mind, yet a mind that thinks through my mind.

God is a being beyond my being, yet a being that is that which I am.

I pray, and in my prayer, I go beyond myself, but not outside myself.

I drink the ocean and I breathe the air, and within myself I find the Infinite—the heart in which I am a heartbeat; the mind in which I am a thought; the being in which I live and move and have my being.

⤐ I sought for God ⤐

Prayer is a search for God.

I have sought for Him.

In my search, I went down many roads. I had many strange encounters. I came on many curious sights.

At last I passed through the desert of denial. In this desert I came to a place where a bush was burning.

The bush sparkled and crackled with flames but was not consumed.

While I stood gazing at this burning bush, a voice spoke out of the midst of it, "Take off your shoes, for this is holy ground."

"I must be very near to God now," I thought.

So I knelt and took off my shoes.

Barefoot I went down that road.

The way led through the plain of temptation. At first it was a land of grassy fields and crystal streams, of fruit and flowers.

But the farther I went, the barer and harder the land became, a rough country where the rocks cut and gashed my feet, so that it hurt more and more to go on.

But after a while a great wind roared up the road. After the wind came an earthquake. After the earthquake came a fire. After the fire came a still small voice.

The voice said, "Remove your robe, for I would see you not as you appear to be but as you are. Thus we will come to know one another."

"I must be very near to God now," I thought.

I removed my robe.

Barefoot and naked I strode through a naked land.

The road led upward through the mountains of hope—green mountains full of trees at first, but the higher I climbed the harder the way became. The rain fell cold on my nakedness. Where the rain ceased, the snow began.

But after a while I came to the top of the mountain.

On the mountaintop were three empty crosses.

Then the clouds parted and out of the clouds came a dove. The dove lit on my shoulder, and a voice said, "Leave your body, for I would make your mind one with my mind, so that there may be between you and me only a clear flow of unobstructed thinking."

"I must be very near to God now," I thought.

So on that mountaintop I left my body.

Barefoot, naked, bodiless, I sprang into the air of aspiration on unencumbered wings of thought. Like an eagle I rose up and up. A wind as from forever caught me and flung me weightless through space. The fierce fires of all the stars burned pitiless into my naked mind, stabbing it with unimagined lightnings—dreams and insights, visions and conjectures. I became bewildered and afraid.

Then in this turbulence a light began to glow. In the light Something moved. This movement was as if a rainbow rippled on itself, and the waves that the rainbow formed were not only light but music, not only music but fragrance, not only fragrance but the touch of a presence, not only a presence but clarity of thought, and the clarity of thought was perfection of mind.

Then out of that perfection of mind a voice said, "Let go of your mind, for myself and yourself must grow to be as one."

"I must be very near to God now," I thought.

So I let go of my mind.

Instantly space and time, form and formlessness, thought and non-thought vanished. Barefoot, naked, bodiless, mindless, I lay outstretched as in a vast abyss. There was no height. There was no depth. There was no beginning. There was no ending. That which I am hung in the emptiness of that which is.

Then in that absolute of silence, in that perfection empty and complete, where I was alone with the Alone, a voice said, "Give up yourself."

Then I saw that I was still alone. I had only emptiness, only silence, only seeking. I was no nearer to God than I had been when I set out on my search.

Then I gave up myself.

Me and mine were no more. That which is more than I stood barefoot, naked, bodiless, mindless, selfless.

But where I had been, God was.

Where my self ended, love's selflessness started.

Then I saw that my bare feet are the feet of God. My naked body is the body of God. My seeking mind is the mind of God. My lonely self is God's unselfishness seeking to give itself to me.

I saw that I was shod. I was clothed. I was in my body. I had my mind. I was myself.

I was going down the road, seeking not God, but man—not so that I might find God but so that I might lose myself in His love.

☙ It is time to pray ❧

I have written a book about prayer. I have written about God, man, and the world. I have written about the prayer that is work, the prayer that is love, the prayer that is submission, the prayer that is discipline, and the prayer that is praise. I have written about the prayer that is not prayer at all.

I have written about the prayer that takes a moment for utterance and the life of prayer.

I have written about the prayer that is a cry for God, and the atheist's prayer.

If I have sometimes seemed to speak in paradoxes and contradictories, this is because the truth of prayer is a many-sided splendor. Truth—I am sure—is a white and single light, brighter than a thousand suns; but the prism of our mind separates it into different colors.

Yet all the contradictories of prayer are resolved—when you pray!—as all the kinds of light become one when you raise your eyes toward the sun.

When you pray, you come to see that you cannot take charge of your thought without putting God in charge of it, and you cannot put God in charge without taking charge yourself.

You cannot work effectively without learning to be still, and you cannot truly be still without working.

You cannot gratify your own desires except by seeking to do God's will, and you cannot seek to do God's will without gratifying your own desires.

When you pray, you not only see these truths, you live these truths. You take charge and you put God in charge. You work and you are still. You do God's will and your needs are met.

So for now, the important thing is not to know all there is to know about prayer. The important thing is to pray—and I have written you out a method of prayer.

It is time, friend, to be at your prayers.

Appendix of Affirmative Prayers

In using the prayers given here, it is well to realize that they are not magic change-alls, intended to work a charm on the universe. They are intended to work a change in you.

When we have a problem, we often go around worrying, depressed, full of fear and anger, expecting the worst to happen. Most of our thoughts are moving us out of harmony, not in harmony with our good. We are wasting, even misusing, the power of our mind and emotions.

When we change this negative pattern; when we set aside definite periods each day to relax, to turn ourselves God-ward, to look for, expect, and affirm our oneness with our good; when, during the day, every time we catch our thought drifting into negation, we take an affirmative prayer like one of these, and deliberately, consciously turn our thought in the direction we want it to take—we are putting our thought-force in harmony with the World-force, with the God-force that is always working for good. We are changing ourselves in ways that cannot help but change our life and our world and bring good to us.

Learn to do this. Form the habit of doing this. And you will find that you have become a new person and that you are living a life of ever-increasing worth, joy, and meaning.

If you are praying for someone else, you can use these prayers by changing the words "I" and "me" to "you."

In Meeting Many Things:

Be still and know that I am God.

Divine order is now established in me through the power of the indwelling Christ.

I am in divine order.

God is in charge.
This is His world.
I am His child.
There are His people.
Now is His time.

God is love. Lovingly in the hands of Love, I place myself.

I am a radiant, all-wise, all-loving, all-conquering son of God. I rule supreme in all the affairs of mind and body.

When you need protection:

The light of God surrounds me;
The love of God enfolds me;
The power of God protects me;
The presence of God watches over me.
Wherever I am, God is!

When you need a sense of life and aliveness:

I love life and life loves to express itself through me.

When you need healing:

God is my health, I am knowing it now.

God is love. God, I relax in Your healing love.

Oh, I am made whole!
Oh, I am made whole!
I am quickened and strengthened
Mind, body, and soul.
Through me now flows the life-stream,
Free its cleansing waves roll—
I enter the current
And I am made whole.

My mind and my heart are attuned to the harmony of the universe. I think and I feel life, life, life.

For a person who is seeking marriage:

There is love in my heart, love in my voice, love in my actions. Giving only love, I attract only love.

When you feel alone and lonely:

Lord of love, let me be a friend when a friend is needed. Let me have a friend when I need a friend.

When you have lost a dear one:

The love of God gives me understanding and the peace that passes understanding. His love bears me up and gives me strength.

When you need to feel at peace about things:

Peace surrounds me and enfolds me. My eyes behold peace. My lips speak peace. My feet walk in paths of peace.

When you feel unjustly treated:

Lord, give me the understanding to be just in all my dealings, and the faith to expect justice and fair treatment.

For one who needs peace of mind, a sense of belonging:

I am peaceful and serene, for I believe life has a meaning and a purpose and I am part of that meaning and purpose.

To help you in business dealings:

All the forces of the universe are working with me, for I am working with God.

When you want to do your work better:

By my positive thoughts, words, and acts I stir up the gifts of God within me and I contribute my best to His good world.

When you need success:

The seed of success is planted in me. With faith it flourishes and brings me a harvest of happiness.

When you are seeking employment:

I thank God I am in my right place, doing my right work in the right way for right pay.

When you need supply or work:

My vision is expanded; my horizon is widened; I recognize and give thanks for unlimited possibilities.

God is my instant, constant, and abundant supply.

*To use as a help in schoolwork, in examinations,
in learning new work:*

I am alert. My mind is quick and I learn easily. I remember perfectly and I express myself freely.

When facing a crisis, making a change:

Fear fades into nothingness; I am filled with courage, for I anticipate only good.

When you need to find a home:

The light of God directs me to my right home right now, and I feel its rightness.

When you have an appointment that is troubling you:

I go to meet my good. I expect the good. I accept the good.

When you need guidance and direction:

I think God-centered thoughts and I am guided into God-directed action.

When you have to meet a loss:

I am no longer burdened with any sense of loss, for I know that nothing goes out of my life except to make room for something better.

When you want to bless someone else:

You are God's child, kept in His love, living His life, doing His work.

I behold the Christ in you.

When you are concerned with another's welfare:

With an understanding heart I feel the needs of those around me, and I express loving faith in their capacity to find the fulfillment of their needs.

To *bless* an *animal:*

God is love. You are part of His love. God is life. You are part of His life. You are the perfect expression of His joy-in-being.